AUTOMATIC UNIVERSE

THE UNIVERSE ACCORDING TO THE MEANING OF LIFE

BY JEFFREY PITTS
non fiction

www.automaticuniverse.com

iUniverse books may be ordered through booksellers or by contacting:

iUniverse
1663 Liberty Drive
Bloomington, IN 47403
www.iuniverse.com
1-800-Authors (1-800-288-4677)

Because of the dynamic nature of the Internet, any Web addresses or links contained in this book may have changed since publication and may no longer be valid. The views expressed in this work are solely those of the author and do not necessarily reflect the views of the publisher, and the publisher hereby disclaims any responsibility for them.

ISBN: 978-1-4502-4248-6 (sc)
ISBN: 978-1-4502-4249-3 (ebook)

Printed in the United States of America

iUniverse rev. date: 06/23/2010

Content Summary

How to read this book
Introduction

Table of Contents

How to read this book

The Automatic Universe is an objective approach toward answering life's most sought-after questions. The goal of the book is to provide you with revelations that bring purpose to the universe. The path to enlightenment is unique for each individual; therefore, *The Automatic Universe* allows you to navigate your own path through the use of "Subject Keys." Subject Keys are sentences that explain the thesis for each topic of discussion. A summary of the Subject Keys is located at the beginning of each section and allows you to choose the most interesting topics based on a subject's thesis. Mark the topics that are relevant to you and follow the path of most interest. The path you have selected will become relevant at the end of the book, where you have the opportunity to enter the path you have selected online to reveal insights into your true nature. Subject keys for each topic are indicated with a Subject Key icon ⌴╫. To get to the point of any topic, locate the Subject Key icon ⌴╫.

The *Automatic Universe* is filled with inspiring quotes from renowned individuals. Several topics are continued on *The Automatic Universe* web site. To access this information and bonus material, use the web site access code below and head to **www.AutomaticUniverse.com**.

More information on the *Automatic Universe* can be found on the website **www.AutomaticUniverse.com**. Our online forum is also available for comments, suggestions, and group discussions. Other media such as videos are posted on the website along with information about book signings and the author's appearance schedule. Copies of the book can be purchased directly from www.AutomaticUniverse.com. If you have questions about the *Automatic Universe* or life in general, email me at jeffrey@automaticuniverse.com, or visit the website and click the "Ask a Guru" button. Talk to me directly on Twitter at **AutomaticU,** or visit my Facebook webpage. You can also watch my video's on YouTube at http://www.youtube.com/automaticu.

Web Site Access Code: automat1cu

Introduction

Every decade introduces a new scientific perspective that changes the way humanity perceives reality. These insights into reality shift the scientific community's direction of study, thereby creating a new paradigm. Paradigms, in turn, usher in inventive ideas about the universe and open doors for successive discoveries. Humanity is predestined to develop science, thereby justifying its place and function within the universe. Humans are inquisitive by nature and seek out the unknown, therein fulfilling ingrained urges to examine the workings of the world. This inquisitive nature has led to discoveries about the universe and humanity itself. The following text will introduce you to the unknown and explain how existence and the universe operate in relation to the human species.

The acquisition of knowledge is on a momentous streak, as science continuously gains intellectual ground upon the workings of existence. This momentum is accompanied by expectations for new discoveries that solve the most sought-after questions about life. Demands for more discoveries build within communities, therein manifesting the emergence of new revelations. The more knowledge and awareness of the universe that is attained, the more questions arise that must be answered. Humanity in the twenty-first century has reached an enlightened pinnacle, a period of insightful inquisition remedied by the introduction of an exotic paradigm. This modern paradigm will usher in a new direction for human progress. An injection of reasoning has long been awaited, which will unify perspectives of existence. The time for absolute reasoning begins its reign upon humanity as waves of understanding and logic melt away questions encroaching upon humanity's nature.

Since the beginning of time, humanity has shaped its world by redefining its surrounding environment. The more humanity is aware of its environment, the more it understands its place and role within it. Everything in humanity's environment has some correlation to the purpose of humans. Without defining this crucial relationship, the pursuit of grasping humanity's purpose becomes dismal. The significance of humanity's environment has little merit unless defined in contrast to humans. The Earth, the solar system, the universe, and everything within it have a critical relationship with humanity. Humanity plays a vital role in the universe, which relates back to the meaning of existence. The meaning of life is the central theme that relates all things within existence and brings purpose to why things are the way they are. Physical principles, the shape of matter, and the roles within society all correlate to the meaning of life. Everything we know relates back to the meaning of life, and without a definitive description of life, all things that exist have little relevance. In order to attach ourselves to this vital role we play in the universe, we must relate all things in existence back to the meaning of life.

The following is a logical examination of existence in relation to humanity. Some of the information provided will come as reassurance for things that are known, while other information will examine the human condition through the eyes of logic. You will discover the meaning of life, humanity, and existence as you gain insight into how the universe and everything within it relates to a single purpose. The material herein will provide insight into your existence and your role in the world. Understanding existence involves the logical examination of what existence represents to humanity. Humanity's role in the universe is a critical one, and the answers to how we will fulfill that role reveals how things operate within existence. The science of why things work the way they do all comes back to the purpose of humanity.

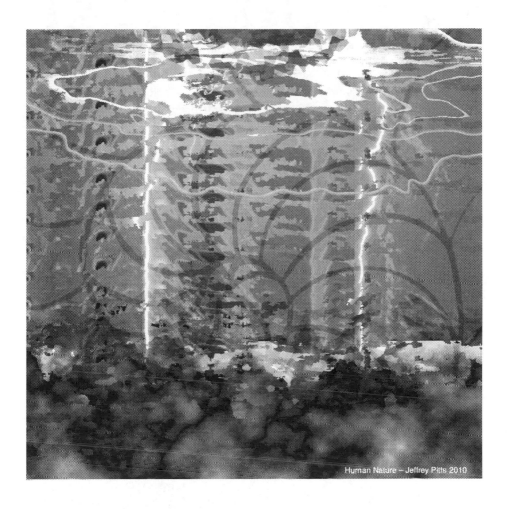

Human Nature – Jeffrey Pitts 2010

Part 1 Humanity and Human Nature

"Man...is a tame or civilized animal never the less, he requires proper instruction and a fortunate nature, and then of all animals he becomes the most divine and most civilized but if he be insufficiently or ill- educated he is the most savage of earthly creatures."

Plato (427 BC - 347 BC), Philosophy

The twenty-first century has left humanity in a precarious frame of mind, balanced on scientific revelations and philosophical enigmas. The windows opened by scientific communities have produced more questions about existence than answers. Still, the great questions facing humanity linger with an ever-greater desire to be resolved. Questions such as *Why is life in the universe negligible, Why is humanity destructive,* and *What is the meaning of existence?* lead us back to the primary question: *Why is everything the way it is?* The more we investigate these questions, the further humanity divides itself from the divine entity that created him. The more humanity explores the stars, the more dismal is the goal of finding answers about man within the vastness of space. *The Automatic Universe* represents a progressive step toward solving humanity's most profound questions.

Humans are aligned with their true nature and operate as they have been intended. Humanity has a purpose, and everything that humans do is in line with that purpose. Humans are an integral component of the universe, so much so that humans are the center of the universe.

1.1 Subject Keys

Choose your path. Read key statements for every topic and mark those topics of most interest. The subject keys that appeal to you reveal insights into your human nature. Read your selections one after another, then move forward to part 4 to discover insights into your nature and how your selections reflect upon you.

KEY STATEMENT	pg
The scope of humanity and its role in relation to existence encompasses everything within the universe as the physical universe becomes humanity's domain. The environmental boundaries of humanity	9
The mind's ability to think exponentially and without restriction presents time as the only catalyst that deters humanity from overcoming every obstacle. An omnipotent creature	11
The cyclical nature of progress ensures that societies advance at fluctuating rates; this leads to cycles of stagnation and then to rapid growth. Man cannot live complacently	12
They are the movers of the world, individuals who accelerate humanity's progress and move it closer to its final goal. Champions of the world	15
The rules of morality apply to the individuals who prescribe to its parameters. Indefinite morality	19
Controlling the thought patterns of the masses is rooted in the process of controlling the experiences the mind absorbs. Deviant behavior	21
In order to control extreme behavior, authoritative figures must impose a level of restrictions. Chaotic and oppressed societies	23
The fluctuating values of life condition the human species, allowing for diverse perspectives that constitute greater achievements. The perceived value of life	26
Humanity is motivated to unravel the unknown in order to limit the burdens brought about by fear. Fear and the unknown	30
The more humanity progresses and advances, the more value it contributes to the universe. You are not living unless you harbor the fear of death	33

1.2 *Human Potential*

The Environmental Boundaries of Humanity

The food chain is comprised of species in order of dominance within a given environment. During one period in history, the human race was not positioned at the top of the food chain, as it is today. Ancient man had to be instinctively aware of predators in order to ensure survival. With the introduction of technology, humans quickly became the dominant species. Humanity's relevance in the food chain diminished with each passing century, as the status of humanity distanced itself from the rest of the animal kingdom. Through progressive revolutions consisting of agriculture, industry, and technology, humanity is becoming less of a component within nature by becoming less dependant on environmental circumstances.

Creatures survive by adapting to their environment. The conditions in a given environment dictate the circumstances a creature must contend with in order to survive. Several creatures are solely reliant upon their habitat and the habitat's ability to supplement life-sustaining substances. Other creatures are able to adapt to multiple environments, maintaining a physical condition capable of conforming to a variety of circumstances. There is an unconventional division in the animal kingdom between those creatures that are subservient to specific environments and those which are unconditionally adaptable to multiple environments. The unconditional creatures are able to adapt to a multitude of environments and maintain a stable vitality when they are displaced. Conditional creatures are solely reliant upon a specific environment for their survival. Displacing these creatures leads to certain extinction. The immediate environment in which a creature exists regulates its potential scope. It limits the creature's functionality specific to a unique environment as it becomes subservient to that environment. However, unconditional creatures conform to several environments and are far less dependent upon a single environment, thereby unlocking an unlimited potential. This ability to master unconventional environments broadens their purpose in relation to existence. Humanity has forged the ability to master several environments, making the purpose of humanity substantial in the grand scheme of existence. As the only unconditionally adaptable creature on Earth, humanity has adopted a remarkable purpose.

Conditions present in a given environment define the scope of the creature in the grand scheme of existence. If a creature is limited to a specific area, the role it plays in relation to existence is limited to that area. Humanity has adapted to several environmental habitats and is no longer restricted to a specific environment. The progress of humanity has led to the mastery of several environments once presumed uninhabitable. The environmental scope in which humanity exists defines the scope of its function in relation to the universe. The scope of humanity surpasses the limits imposed by Earth and extends beyond the physical universe. Humanity's role in the universe becomes considerably grander, as humanity explores uninhabited areas in space. Humanity's habitual environment has become the physical limits of the universe. ⊐⊢⊩ The scope of humanity and its role in relation to existence encompasses everything within the universe, as the physical universe becomes humanity's domain. Humanity's ability to master any environment extends humanity's role beyond any limits of the physical universe.

Instruments bestowed upon the human body allow humans to master multiple environments. The refinement of the body through evolution has accommodated humanity with an "all terrain chassis" capable of traversing several environments. The one instrument that defines humanity's versatility is the mind, as the mind's ingenuity has become the only limitation toward mastering increasingly exotic environments. Possessing unlimited possibilities, the mind contains the capacity to overcome obstacles that limit humanity to Earth's environment. Physical environmental limitations dissolve in the wake of human contemplation, as the boundless mind bestows humanity with an unlimited scope. The mind has the ability to think progressively in an infinite capacity. This ability differentiates humans from other species and broadens humanity's scope with the passing of time.

An Omnipotent Creature

A hierarchy of aspirations classifies the degrees of human achievement. The more paramount achievements are positioned higher on the hierarchy, compared to those achievements with minimal merit. Those who aspire to great things are notably rewarded, while those with few accomplishments or aspirations are less notable and fall under the classification of mediocrity. Every person has the potential to aspire to be great or to dissolve into mediocrity. As humanity progresses, the possibility of greater achievements through the utilization of accumulative knowledge is more readily attainable. The progress of man leads to the possibility of attaining greater feats beyond the accomplishments of previous generations. Humanity progressively raises the bar of achievement with each generation.

There are abilities of man that are presently unknown to him beyond that of commonality. As humanity matures, humans are able to contemplate grander thoughts and schemes. The limitations restricting superior achievements dissolve with time, as the mind is able to contemplate grander thoughts through the utilization of greater knowledge. Obstacles once presumed impossible to overcome are conquered with the passing of time. Limitations and obstacles become opportunities for future generations to overcome. Obstacles become temporary obstructions dealt with in the passage of time. The mind's limitless capacity only requires time to mature, therein acquiring the ability to resolve future dilemmas. Humanity's ability to comprehend innovative knowledge is the only catalyst impeding his progress. □┤-┼┤ The mind's ability to think exponentially and without restriction presents time as the only catalyst that deters humanity from overcoming every obstacle. As the mind matures, humanity is moving toward the omnipotent creature it was designed to be. Each surmounted obstacle becomes a testament to humanity's place in the universe and humanity's path toward becoming an omnipotent creature.

Man Cannot Live Complacently

Humanity is constantly growing and evolving in a positive direction. This inevitable progression is by design, fuelled by the reluctant will of man. Man cannot live complacently. The constant struggle of life pushes civilizations toward advancements leading to natural progression. Desires instilled in man lead him to fulfill a void that is never ending and relentless. Devices programmed into the design of man ensure a gradual positive progression. Aggressive human ambitions have fuelled wars that have transformed environments, resulting in advancements in technology and social engineering. These aggressive behaviors and motivations comprise the fundamental features of humanity that nurture its desire to progress.

There are cycles of progression, like seasons, that manipulate the rate of human progress. Humanity's progress does falter periodically, causing regressions in the rate of progress. There are sags within human progression when humanity's growth becomes stagnant. These are conditions under which humanity experiences instances of complacency that eventually lead to events of rapid growth. The cycle of progression ensures that periods of stagnate growth do not continue indefinitely. The cycles dictate the rate of progression much like the momentum of a pendulum, decreasing and increasing the velocity of the pendulum's bob given its position. This fluctuating rate mimics the movement described in the *rebound effect,* where every occurrence of negative growth has a reaction of a doubling positive growth. This cause and effect creates an accumulating positive rate of progression, enabling humanity to climb the ladder of human evolution. Therefore, a substantial period of negative growth will result in an enormous period of positive growth.

Conditions in any society are constantly changing, as change is the primary component of progress. Like the changing of the seasons, a society experiences cycles in the rate of progress. Modern conveniences have increased the quality of life and have made living very comfortable to such a degree that subsequent generations have become less ambitious and more complacent. The progressive struggle of society to become proficient inevitably leads to its stagnation. These occurrences arise during the peak of a society's success and inevitably lead to its downfall. The foregone collapse ensures that humanity is constantly evolving at an accelerated pace, thereby avoiding extended periods of complacency.

Societies differ in their rate of progression because progress is conditional upon the circumstances of the society's inhabitants. Societies that exhibit idealistic circumstances for development will surpass the rates of progression of those societies that have eclipsed their peak *progression performance*. Striving nations ultimately maintain higher rates of progress over complacent ones. The potential for growth and advancement is greater in striving nations, as the population is instilled with a sense of urgency to improve its circumstance. The cyclical nature of progress ensures that a society cannot maintain a high rate of progress indefinitely. As stagnant societies regress into complacency, other societies backed by the impeding will of man surpass the progression rates once held by dominant societies. The cyclical nature of progress ensures that complacent societies will eventually rebound to return to competitive rates of progress. Conditions will arise wherein stagnant societies will become agitated, dislodged from the confines of their comfortable stasis, and return to their progressive stature. □—HI The cyclical nature of progress ensures that societies advance at fluctuating rates; this leads to cycles of stagnation and then rapid growth.

Figure 1   Progression and complacency

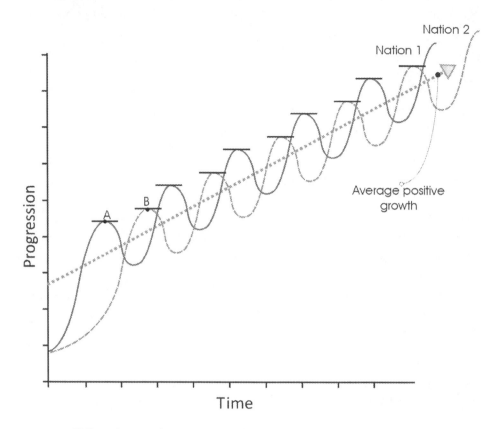

When humanity as a whole reaches a *progression peak*, it will regress into complacency, thereby producing circumstances that will inevitably inflict great change, causing humanity to become highly progressive. Stagnant societies, those that are unchanging and not advancing, are deemed unfit for survival and positively rebound in growth in order to avoid extinction. Examples of these conditions can be found throughout history in patterns of growth and collapse of a civilization. The cycle of progression will empower those nations that embody growth by staying in a state of activity and innovation. It will corrode those nations that neglect rapid growth and that become complacent. Dominant nations eventually decline, imploding upon their success as they are unable to sustain momentous growth. With struggle comes progress; without struggle, complacency sets in and decays the society in preparation for its momentous rebound. These are the cyclical laws of nature that dictate the progress of humanity. Figure 1 illustrates the positive progressive cycle of two nations. When nation 1 becomes complacent (position A), it reaches a progression plateau. The other struggling nation, nation 2, builds momentum and surpasses the advancement of the competing nation (position B), only to reach an inevitable stagnant plateau. As nations trump each other, the inevitable progress of humanity accumulates in a positive directional arrow.

Champions of the World

The pursuit of a fulfilled life is a constant undertaking. Humans gain pleasure and fulfillment through a variety of venues that exert varying degrees of reward. The greater the potential fulfillment, the more desirable the activity becomes and the more vigorously it is pursued. Humans cherish some desires more than others by design. We are instinctively willed to pursue the pleasures that are the most satisfying. For instance, notoriety yields a high-ranking reward and therefore is highly pursued. Movie stars receive great satisfaction when they are at the top of their profession.

The pursuit of fulfillment leads to personal achievement, for it is through the process of acquiring fulfillment that an individual rises above mediocrity. Excelling over and above others brings a great sense of achievement and fulfillment. This pursuit of fulfillment is instilled within humans and is implanted in our desires. If we pursue our greatest desires, we are following the embedded code planted within us by design. When we follow our natural course of desire, we are following the purposeful path set out by our designers.

Those who live a purposeful life have attained a high degree of fulfillment. The process of attaining this fulfillment influences not only the pursuer but also those who recognize the process for what it is. The pursuer becomes the champion, rising above mediocrity and influencing humanity. The champions of the world are those who have brought about the most change or influence upon humanity, whether it is perceived as positive or negative. ☐─╫╫ They are the movers of the world, individuals who accelerate humanity's progress and move it closer to its final goal. The movers are those individuals who are the most satisfied in life, as they receive the greatest sense of fulfillment. The individuals who have affected, influenced, and changed the most people reap the greatest rewards. For instance, displacing humanity causes measures of change that nature automatically rewards. The result of this change is the inevitable accelerated growth and progress of the human species. Growth is essentially about change to any degree and the elimination of stagnation.

The universe adheres to the process of growth and movement; everything we perceive in the universe is constantly in motion and the farther out into space we look, the faster things are moving. In an effort to remain aligned with this facet, humanity is constantly in motion. Those who cause change or motion are aligned with the cause of the universe. The greater the agitation inflicted upon humanity, the more change and growth will occur as a result.

We should praise the movers for the changes they bring onto humanity, and label each influence as an achievement to human progress. The shakers of the world should be held in high esteem. The movers reap greater rewards for their efforts, and this perpetuates their desire for greater achievements. Figure 2 depicts the lifetimes of individuals M and L. M attains greater fulfillment in
a shorter period of time than L. Individual L attains his maximum fulfillment at point F, nearing the end of his lifetime. Individual M achieves the same fulfillment during a shorter period of time, thus making M a "mover." M achieves the highest level of fulfillment at point G, a point where L cannot attain (line H). Individual M lives a fulfilled life with greater purpose and achievement.

16

Figure 2   Change and Rewards

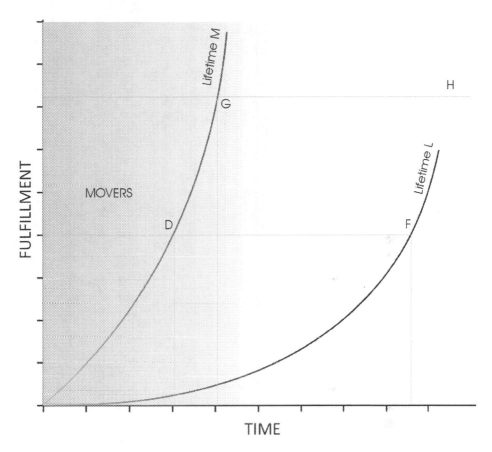

D - Mid fulfillment for lifetime M
F - High fulfillment for lifetime L
G - High fulfillment for lifetime M
H - Unreachable fulfillment lifetime L

Society at an End

> *"A state is not a mere society, having a common place, established for the prevention of mutual crime and for the sake of exchange...Political society exists for the sake of noble actions, and not of mere companionship."*
>
> Aristotle (384 BC - 322 BC), Politics

Indefinite Morality

Morality is a characteristic attributed to and conditioned by humans. The standards defining morality vary between countries, societies, and individuals. The definition of morality for an individual is based upon an individual's experiential state. There are no fixed standards or baselines for defining the conditions of morality, as the notion itself is subject to human judgment. The conditions for morality change with time and circumstances, rendering its definition subjective. The definition of morality is therefore biased, as one society will perceive the parameters regulating morality differently from another society. For example, one society may perceive war as morally just, while another will view it as a squandering of resources. Both societies are correct in their assessment, even though the opinions are polar opposites. The morality practiced by one group should not be imposed upon other groups with conflicting perceptions of morality. One standard of morality is not superior over another and should not dictate the criteria by which all moral standards are judged.

Morality can only be accepted by those willing to abide by its principles. ☐╫ The rules of morality apply to the individuals who prescribe to its parameters. An individual lives up to the standards of morality that he or she endorses. Individuals follow the principles of their own perception of morality attained from experiential conditions expressed within their society. If an individual lives in a society that holds morality with high prestige, the individual will more likely adopt a similar perception.

The standards of morality cannot be defined under a universal context because the definition depends upon the human condition. A universal standard of morality is impossible to describe, as each opinion will vary from the next. Morality, among other human traits, should be critiqued upon how it applies to the nature of the species. The study of morality, or ethics, is the examination of humanity in relation to the parameters of morality. It is the examination of how the species creates morals and uses them to justify their actions. Human nature requires us to be irate and collective, immoral and moral, judgmental and compassionate. It is in our nature to be a degree of these conditions. Whether we are acting on one characterization rather than another, we are rightfully doing so by our nature. The one true universal precedence enunciates that nature cannot be wrong; therefore, our actions are always right. For example, the head lion of a lion's pride kills its cubs to preserve its reign. This action can be perceived as immoral and murderous, but by the laws of nature, the lion is doing what it was programmed to do. Humans follow the same universal precedents, so that if our actions are done in the course of our nature, they are done rightfully. There are no questions of morality, as actions are conducted within the confines of human nature. The extent to which human actions are judged as "moral" is strictly based on opinions and not conditioned under universal contexts.

Human actions that are subject to moral standards should be judged less upon a given standard of morality and more upon the circumstances leading to them. Actions are conducted based on a series of events leading to an inevitable decision. There is a science behind every decision that makes the conclusion inevitable, given the sequential circumstances leading to an action. Human actions should be analyzed rather than criticized. Actions should be studied analytically, examining motives and circumstances leading to decisions. This type of analysis is similar to the conduct of investigators at a crime scene, but also applies to mundane human events. The majority of actions are based upon a complicated series of events and circumstances, which makes it unwieldy to define the logic behind those decisions. The variables involved in one human decision may be overwhelming, making the study of decision making unscientific. Judgments are classified as coincidental, which gives rise to the assumption that human behavior is random. The more complex the circumstances behind a decision is, the more random an action will appear.

Deviant Behavior

The mind is an interactive utility that stores and processes experiences. Experiences absorbed by the mind contort the mind's thought processing mechanisms. Minds that absorb similar experiences have similar thought processes and think alike. Thought processes are unique among individuals, as each mind contains uniquely stored experiences. Experiences cannot be perceived identically, which gives rise to individuality and unique thinking. The variety of experiences acquired by the mind can be attributed to the uniqueness of each individual. The closer the experiences absorbed by two minds, the closer the thought processing patterns within the minds will be. In order to determine the mind's characteristics, one should determine the experiences stored within the mind. Deciphering the experiences absorbed by the mind involves examining thought patterns and reactions produced by the host maintaining the mind. These instinctive processes expose the types of experiences housed in the mind and unfold classifications for behavior. For instance, unique minds project distinguished attributes that are conveyed through decisions and actions. These actions in turn become the looking glass into the mind, projecting the host's thought processing patterns.

Individuals living in close proximity often share similar experiences and develop similar thought processes. For instance, inseparable siblings think alike and finish each other's sentences.

Similar findings can be observed among individuals in secluded communities. Citizens of metropolises who are exposed to a common media often exhibit similar personas and behaviors. ☐–╫ Controlling the thought patterns of the masses is rooted in the process of controlling the experiences absorbed by the mind. Manipulating thought processes entails monopolizing the experiences of the mind with selective content. The influence of a mainstream media creates a social segregation between citizens of one society and people from foreign societies.

People who have been isolated from mainstream social media develop thought processing patterns alien to social norms. These individuals are perceived as abnormal, as their behavior does not coincide with social benchmarks. Obsessive behavior is a trait characterized by thinking thoughts outside typical social norms. Obsessive behavior is a deviation from mainstream social psychology and is developed by the exposure to alien experiences that obscure the mind's thought processing patterns. Conditions such as sociological deprivation and exposure to abnormal experiences bring upon deviant behavior. These abnormal experiences are more readily adopted during adolescence, for an inexperienced mind is more susceptible to abnormal influences. The mind can easily be influenced and conform to uncommon behavior; therefore, children are often protected from exposure to abnormal experiences in order to ensure that they adjust to the social norms.

The intellectual elite are characterized as having conditions of obsession. Those subjected to deviant experiences tend to sustain degrees of obsessive behavior. A common trait among the intellectual elite is that they have experienced conditions of disorder in their lives, a purge from the complacent life. Deviations from social norms can produce positive attributes that heighten an individual's abilities. To have strived for greatness is to have undergone a state of deprivation from normal living. The story of Adam and Eve first introduces the concept of breaking from the norm for personal gain. Once they bit the forbidden fruit, a painful change gave rise to human achievement. Achievement is the process of purging oneself from the norm.

Deprivation from complacent living will give rise to obsession and opportunities for substantial achievement.

Chaotic and Oppressed Societies

The practice of controlling societal behavior entails controlling the experiences absorbed by the society. Influencing societal behavior is therefore rooted in the dilemma of manipulating thought patterns and the way the mind processes thoughts. The mind is a boundless device, an experience-absorbing databank conforming to external influences. The practice of manipulating an individual's mind is not a precise science, as minds are complex and are not all the same. There are fundamental conditions that must be met before one can initiate mind manipulation. These conditions ensure that the majority of minds in a society will be influenced. In order to impose these conditions, the mind has to be tentative and responsive to influences, and the individual must be obedient to the medium conveying the influences. This seduction is often spearheaded through the practice of societal suppression, a process that conditions groups to be obedient in order to impose external influences. In order to control the masses, an element of suppression must be imposed upon a society.

Governing agencies constantly manipulate regulations and laws in order to optimize the behavioral dispositions within societies. The refining of laws involves tightening or relaxing restraints in order to sustain a degree of social order. Without a proper balance, social order will become unstable. A society is entangled between two behavioral conditions that regulate social order; these include oppressive behavior and chaotic behavior. Depending on the level of restraints placed upon a society, citizens will exhibit one of these conditions more than the other. Given the amount of suppression imposed by the government, the society's behavioral state will sway from one condition to another. Government restrictions imposed on societies are a component of the social order designed to control social interactions by keeping societal behavior within acceptable levels.

Authoritative figures are present in abundance during the course of any human's life, and certain behaviors are suppressed by these authoritative figures during the different stages of life. An authority for regulating human behavior is required, as human behavior can be unpredictable. In order to mitigate actions caused by sporadic behavior, restrictions are imposed to make people comply with social norms. Examples of authoritative figures are evident within everyday society and illustrate the requirement for a chain of command. From corporate structures to Third World tribes, authoritative figures mitigate the allowable actions of their followers. Human behavior is capable of fluctuating to extremes; thus the imposed baseline restrictions keep sporadic behaviors subdued. Humanity, by nature, has sporadic tendencies, a design imposed to condition its progress. Restrictions are imposed by authorities who limit these extremes and reinforce social norms. ⬚┼╫ In order to control extreme behavior, authoritative figures must impose a level of restriction. Human nature is programmed to exploit resources, and this exploitation will relentlessly commence unless there is something in place to suppress these actions. Without restrictions or suppression, humanity would relentlessly exploit resources. Restrictions regulate behavior and limit those who would purge society of its norms.

Regulations imposed upon society require constant refinement as social circumstances fluctuate. The task bestowed upon governing agents is to restore the desired balance of social order demanded by society. This process partially consists of mitigating restrictions that often become unbalanced, thereby causing social upheaval. Increased restrictions lead to oppressed societies and as a result cause a physiological state of low self-esteem. A balance must be retained between suppression and impartiality in order to sustain practical social behavior. These devices prevent society from resorting to chaotic or oppressed extremes. Figure 3 displays the behavioral state and self-worth of a society with various levels of suppression imposed upon it. Point A depicts a state of low suppression, which causes high self-worth and empowers the society, leading to a people-led state. Points B and C define the average states of societal suppression that lead to a government-controlled society. Point D defines high suppression, causing low self-worth and leading to an oppressed society. In order to achieve optimal social order, governing agents impose restrictions to maintain a society's behavioral patterns within Points B and C.

Figure 3   Controlling The Masses With Suppression

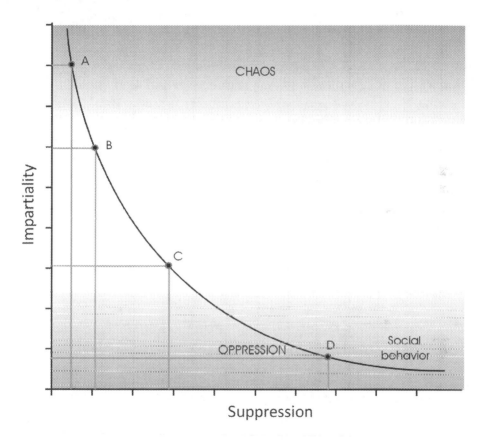

A - High rebellion, low suppression = a chaotic nation
B - Moderate rebellion = a people-governed nation
C - Moderate suppression = a government-controlled nation
D - High suppression, low rebellion = an oppressed nation

The Perceived Value of Life

The perceived value of life influences a society's behavior and psychology. Life is perceived as a commodity, and its value is weighed against other commodities. The basic laws of supply and demand dictate the general perception of a commodity's value. Life's value is unique; therefore, it is highly regulated and controlled by governing agents. Citizens decide upon the value of life by consensus, which is then conveyed to governing agents, who implement laws to protect these values. The values influence several social facets, including crime, health, suicide, morality, population growth, and economic progress. Governments continually optimize life's value to control social order and ensure economic stability.

The ideal values of life rarely sway to extremes. Implementing extreme ideologies toward the value of life is neither suitable nor constructive for human progress. The optimal realized value of life, which promotes stability, lies between the extremes. For instance, if the value of life were considered low, conflicts and wars would ensue over materials that were perceived to have greater value. If it were considered too high, progress would deflate and the preservation of man would be the focal point of society while other explorations and advancements in economies would cease. The optimal value of life lies within the balance between the extremes, fluctuating with little variance.

Civilized societies place a higher value on life than on other commodities. As civilizations mature, the value placed on life increases. The demand for commodities decreases as advancements in technology and knowledge create ample supplies of material goods. People are able to attain greater amounts wealth and therefore have more to lose from the loss of life. Investments in education and health increase, as people invest in their own well-being and in the population at large. The society places a higher priority on the welfare of individuals and dedicates a larger portion of government grants toward human development. In addition, punishments for crimes against life increase in severity in order to deter criminal acts against life. The parameters defining morality and civil behavior are amplified in stature and become a part of government regulations.

The value of life is constantly fluctuating and is never constant. Values within a society fluctuate as citizens interact and experience events outside the norm. It is the responsibility of the government to standardize the perceived value of life in order to establish a baseline that reflects social norms. Although governments maintain rigid regulations concerning life, populations abiding by these regulations may hold dissimilar values. Although these values can be dissimilar, variances do not stray far from the projected baseline. Civilized societies perceive the value of life as the most valued commodity in relation to other commodities, and those who preserve this value are praised as society's heroes. Popular culture promotes the sanctity of life, but this ideology can be taken to extremes, which becomes detrimental to a society. ⬜┼╢ The fluctuating values of life condition the human species, allowing for diverse perspectives that constitute greater achievements. For instance, when faced with less than ideal perspectives on life's value, citizens are willing to take risks that may result in substantial gains.

Life's value tends to retract to baseline levels when pushed to extremes. If the value sharply increases or decreases in relation to social norms, a society's reflex is to restore the value to a tolerable position. During periods of a depleted perception of life, humanity will instinctively strive to improve the value assessment. During levels of positive assessments, a mature society strives to normalize the value to tolerable levels. Therefore, humanity is constantly striving to normalize the value of life.

Figure 4 depicts the perceived value of life for two societies and their tendencies to normalize the value of life. Society B is a mature society with a peak perceived value of life at Point J. Point J reflects a social climate of low crime, adequate health services, and minimal suicides; the value of life exceeds that of other commodities (commodity equilibrium). Society B inflicts high penalties upon those who violate laws that protect life. Crime is treated with harsh penalties, health systems are held to high standards, social programs

27

are relevant and mandatory, and healthy living programs are promoted. With a higher value of life ingrained in Society B's psyche, citizens treat their bodies as sacred and are willing to go beyond normal measures to optimize their physical condition.

Figure 4   Social Forming and the Value of Life

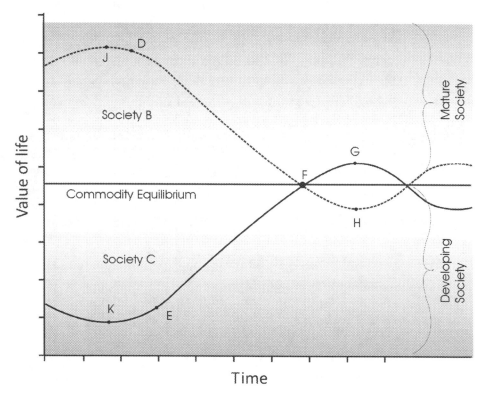

Time

A society consumed with the perception of a high value of life does not operate optimally, as the majority of its focus is concentrated on the preservation of life. Negative aspects found in Society B include sciences focusing on medicine and ways to preserve life instead of focusing on new technologies outside the health industry. Industries decay when subject to limited improvements in manufacturing, and the society as a whole becomes complacent and dependent on the dated technology. Point D depicts a decrease in the perceived value of life as the demand for commodities inflates. The ideal value of life becomes relaxed as Society B is exposed to events that destabilize the normal perception. This decrease in the perceived value is within acceptable boundaries of the social norms and allows standards to sink to Point F. The tolerable level of the new perception reaches a breaking point, triggering a reaction from Society B. The values of other commodities have reached a comparable value to that of life, and this is a notion that the society is unwilling to accept. Society B reaches the least acceptable perceived value of life at Point F. As the value sinks lower, the comfort level becomes intolerable, causing more citizens to react. The accumulated reaction of the society changes the momentum of the perceived value at Point H, which ultimately causes the value to increase.

Society C resides in a developing country that places a low value on life (Point K). Developing societies have few human regulations, and the value of other commodities typically takes precedence over human life. Events in Society C have caused the perceived value of life to increase to Point E, eventually reaching the echelons of a mature society at Point F. Society C reaches its highest point for the perceived value of life at Point G, but then quickly reverts to a more normalized level below the commodity equator. Society C is a commodity-driven economy wherein the society is unable to sustain a constant high value of life due to the scarcity of commodities. As the value of life increases, the economy suffers (Point G), thereby retracting the value back to tolerable levels.

The perceived value of life is unique between cities, towns, and individuals. Individuals perceive varying values of life based on their personal circumstances and experiences. Greater interaction within a population leads to a more mainstream perception for the perceived value of life. In large, condensed populations, life's value is constantly measured, thereby fluctuating more rapidly leading to less subjective interpretations of values. Perceptions in rural areas are more diverse and are susceptible to erratic fluctuations due to lesser social interaction.

Fear and the Unknown

A series of emotions are induced when humans become excited. In such instances, emotions fluctuate and trigger an array of responses. These emotions can be fearful or gratifying, thereby willing humans to be inquisitive. Discovering new phenomena is an important part of human nature, as intelligent beings require explanations for the unknown in order to appease their inquisitive minds. The mind is a human's greatest tool, and it continually strives to absorb new and unique experiences. The mind uses these experiences to compose unique ideas by amalgamating experiences into thoughts. The mind is a powerful tool that has not been fully exploited. Left to its own devices, the mind can conjure emotionally induced experiences that mimic reality. The power of the mind can bring fantasies into perceived reality, and therefore it must be tamed. But taming the mind requires logic, reasoning, and explanations of reality to limit the mind's capacity to create surreal realities. Without these restrictions, the mind's internal mechanisms can induce fear to protect a subject from the unknown. The more one knows, the more in control he or she is, and the less there is to fear. □─┼┼ Humanity is motivated to unravel the unknown in order to limit the burdens brought about by fear.

As we grow older, our experiences with the physical world reduce the amount of fear we once harbored as children. Children have a heightened sense of fear as they are more susceptible to unknown experiences and therefore are more vulnerable. Guardians teach children what is and is not harmful, thereby curtailing their fearful nature. As childish fears diminish, new fears are acquired in adulthood as the mind gains the ability to comprehend new realities. For instance, at a certain stage in life, the realization that not everything can be explained induces another sort of fear. The acquisition and removal of fears continually fluctuates throughout life, ultimately improving the human experience. Exposure to unique realities induces peaks and valleys of fear.

Humanity has consistently set out to define the unknown, thereby reducing its dependency on myths, gods, and folklore. The ultimate delimiter for appeasing the mind is the knowledge that there

30

is some logic controlling phenomena that cannot be mastered by man. When things are out of our control, fear and chaos ensue. It would be a relief to know that the ride of life is completely safe, providing us with thrills but never endangering us. This conclusion can never be realized, as it would change the definition of the human experience. The ability to experience fear of the unknown provides humanity with unique situations that stimulate the experience of life. It is a crucial component of the human experience.

1.4　*Life and Death*

> *"If you don't get what you want, you suffer; if you get what you don't want, you suffer; even when you get exactly what you want, you still suffer because you can't hold on to it forever. Your mind is your predicament. It wants to be free of change. Free of pain, free of the obligations of life and death. But change is a law, and no amount of pretending will alter that reality."*
>
> Dan Millman, The Way of the Peaceful Warrior

You Are Not Living Unless You Harbor the Fear of Death

There are expectations and responsibilities attributed to living things in the universe. Elements with responsibilities perform a role in the grand scheme of existence and thus attain a degree of importance. Life retains an intrinsic value; this value is accumulated and credited to the total intrinsic value of the universe. The universe maintains an intrinsic value that equals the aggregated intrinsic value of all the entities that exist within it. The more complex an organism is, the greater the intrinsic value it attributes to the universe. Likewise, the less effort required to explain an organism's function in relation to the universe, the less value it retains in the grand scheme. The complexity of the universe is reflected by the amount of intrinsic value it maintains. The investments made in time, refinements, and improvements of elements within the universe contribute to a greater intrinsic value. As the universe grows, it increases its intrinsic value.

The significance of an organism in relation to its function within the universe determines its degree of intrinsic value. The life of a human requires a more elaborate definition than that of a single-celled organism. There are simple explanations for the existence of plants, but the human species has a far more complicated explanation. This complexity stems from humanity's unique role and responsibility in the universe. Intrinsic values vary between species, but humanity is the most complex, so it has the greatest value. Intrinsic values represent the level of importance in association to existence, as they determine an entity's worth.

The greater the purpose and responsibility imposed upon a species, the more worth it attains. The human species contains several characteristics that make it the predominant entity in the universe. A human's self-awareness is a dominant component attributable to humanity's intrinsic value. The ability to master thought gives humanity a value that surpasses all other species. Humanity's intrinsic value eclipses the value of other entities to such an extent that the majority of the universe's value is represented by humanity. Every human advancement adds profound value to the universe. □┤╫ The more humanity progresses and advances, the more value it contributes to the universe.

The universe has invested more resources into the production of humanity than any other organism, making humanity's degree of intrinsic value greater than other entities. The intrinsic value of humanity as a whole influences the intrinsic value of the universe to such an extent that the death of a significant human immensely diminishes the universe's value. The individual intrinsic value of each human varies, with select individuals retaining more value than others. A single human life does not have any worth unless it contributes to the grand scheme of the universe. Those whose lives excel and propel humanity to its ultimate goal retain a higher value. Figure 5 shows the associated value of humanity in relation to other living organisms. Those organisms that contribute more to the universe attain a higher position on the chart. These substantial organisms can accomplish greater feats toward the attainment of the universe's end. The more an individual contributes to the ultimate goal of humanity, the greater the value associated with him. Individuals contributing less have less value and are, subsequently, on par with less significant organisms like plants and other animals. Individuals who accelerate humanity's progress have more value than an average human does. The sensation of living is greatest when one's value exceeds that of the average human. You are not living unless you are captivated by the fear of losing your value if you die.

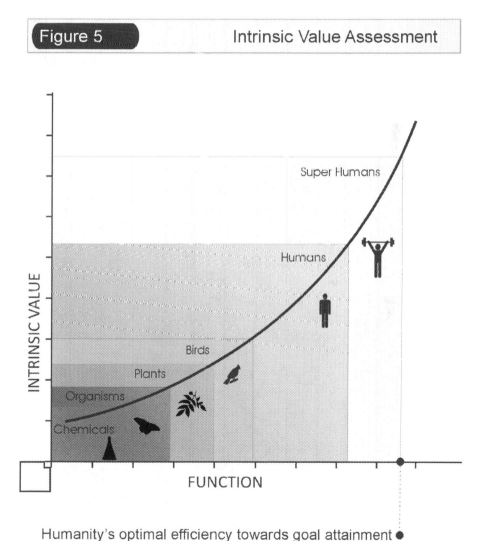

Figure 5   Intrinsic Value Assessment

Humanity's optimal efficiency towards goal attainment ●

Fear versus the Value of Life

The emotion of fear is triggered by experiences that pose potential harm. Humans are programmed to fear and are also taught what to fear. There are several devices in society that teach us what to fear. Fear is induced by an instinctive reaction, a defensive mechanism that helps us avoid potential harm. The greater the potential harm, the more fear we experience. Fears subside in various magnitudes during different stages of life. Childhood is the process of learning what is to be feared. Children learn from their guardians how to react to certain situations, therein testing their fear thresholds. To ensure their survival, children's fears are intensified as they rely upon guardians for their protection. This sensitive defensive mechanism causes children to react dramatically in the face of potential harm.

The perception of fear changes as humans graduate from childhood to adulthood. A clearer understanding of what is potentially harmful is adopted, including an understanding of the consequences from fearful experiences. The ultimate consequence, death, induces the most amount of fear, while other consequences may be sustained and therefore induce less fear. Death is the ultimate loss an individual can sustain in the physical world, as everything the individual has experienced or will experience is taken away at that point. Losses may be measured in relation to the value of life. Individuals with a high value of life or great potential for achievement have more to lose. The realization of this loss induces more fear within the subject, as they are more motivated to stay alive and avoid harm. For example, teenagers have little concept of the value or potential of their lives, therefore they are more willing to risk their lives. With minimal insight into the value of their lives, death becomes less of a deterrent to their ambitions.

Adulthood brings upon a clearer understanding of the value of life and what is to be feared. During adulthood, a life's potential is realized and the accumulation of wealth begins. Fear becomes less about what harm can be done to an individual and more about what an individual would lose if harm should occur. With an acute understanding of life's worth, a person understands the degree of harm that can be tolerated. The accumulated value of life at a certain stage of life is weighed, and the greater the value, the greater the potential loss. Individuals take more precautions if they place a high value on life. Adults who are unaware of the value of their lives have less to fear and take fewer precautions than those who are more aware of their inherent value. ⬚–⫯⫯ Fear has more of an impact on those who are aware of the potential value of their lives.

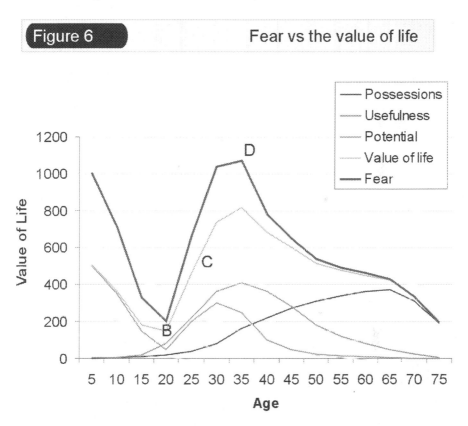

Figure 6   Fear vs the value of life

Old age returns an individual to a vulnerable state, making them once more dependent on others for survival. With the potential of life diminished, the total value of life decreases; this, in turn, causes fear to become less potent. Figure 6 displays the relationship between the value of life and the degree of fear an individual harbors. The value of life is attributed to a conglomeration of values, including possessions, usefulness, and potential. Fear decreases in childhood and reaches a minimum at Point B, where the realized value of life is at its lowest. Fear continues to climb (Point C) as the value of life increases and reaches a peak, at Point D. The potential value of life decreases drastically as people near the end of their lives, thus reducing the potency of their fear. These values fluctuate between subjects, but generally follow a common pattern throughout life.

Immortality

The concept of immortality is associated with infinities, timelessness, and eternity. In reference to humanity, it represents eternal life. Immortality has been one of mankind's goals since its conception. Civilizations have built religions and cultures based on the concept of immortality and the continuation of life. Evidence from ancient civilizations have shown attempts to achieve immortality. Legendary religious figures portrayed as defying death can be found in many cultures. Death is one of the lasting, defying obstacles that man has minimal control over. Immortality holds more intrigue for those nearing death.

The concept of immortality and its attainment is ingrained within human programming. A fundamental component within man manifests a desire to exist forever. This desire is natural, as it is the craving to fulfill a void found in all humans. The traditional method of achieving a sense of immortality is through procreation. The persona and name of an individual is passed on through subsequent generations, thereby keeping alive the memories of those who created them. This method is quite contrary to conventional portrayals of immortality commonly depicted in popular media. Conventional immortality entails a conscious being's self-preservation of his or her mortal existence. The conflicting concept in this scenario is the inability of matter to maintain a fixed condition. Mortal objects are susceptible to change, whereas immortality entails an unchanging, utopian existence. These concepts exist on separate plateaus, as they contradict each other.

All physical matter changes and therefore eludes immortality. The one constant entity unsusceptible to change is thought. An idea, concept, or principle can exist forever through thought. Things exist forever in our minds, unsusceptible to change, aging, or degradation. Principles or physical laws are examples of immortal concepts. Physical principles are rehearsed in the minds of humanity while maintaining their prestige. Humanity's glamorization of immortality has portrayed material objects as mystically existing forever. Living forever is not a physical endeavor, but rather a mental venture. Infinity only exits in the realm of the mind. ☐⊦⊦⊦ Rising from the world beyond entails one's essence existing in everyday human life through thought. One's ideas, thoughts, work, and methodologies are remembered and rehearsed by the living. Those who remember and take action in your name create your immortality. Our actions in the mortal world take precedence in maintaining an individual's immortality, as legacies retain immortality. A person's eternal existence depends upon the actions of future generations in their regard.

Those who are remembered are individuals who have risen from obscurity and have had a substantial influence upon humanity. The greater the change imposed upon humanity, the more notoriety attained and influence gained. Becoming immortal entails effecting the greatest changes and influences on Earth. The greatest reign of immortality is achieved when all of humanity acknowledges your existence. Building temples, monuments, religions, and civilizations are humanity's attempts to live forever. The ancient Egyptians attempted immortality by building everlasting temples and recording their stories on limestone to transcend generations. The assurance for immortality was gained when greater temples were erected and memorable stories were conjured. The resurrection of ancient Egyptian kings entails man re-enacting their legacy, thereby maintaining their immortality.

The Meaning of Life

> *"I see many people die because they judge that life is not worth living. I see others paradoxically get in killed for the ideas or illusions that give them a reason for living (what is called a reason for living is also an excellent reason for dying). I therefore conclude that the meaning of life is the most urgent of questions."*
>
> Albert Camus (1913 - 1960), The Myth of Sisyphus

The Universe Requires Change

Humans are one of many components in the universe, equal to the same standings of other components. The stars we see in the night sky contain substances similar to those found in us, only composed differently. Humanity shares common attributes with other components, as all things were created by the same inventor and have originated from the same substance. The blueprints used to create man are evident in the composition of other things the inventor has created. Humanity shares a common underlying trait with all other components. All of these components in the universe reveal insights into their creator's intent. This conceptual intention is embedded within humanity and has been passed down through generations, revealing insights into the consciousness of the inventor. We can sense this grounding will of the inventor when we concentrate on our desires. By focusing on our essential motives, we are tapping into the desires of the universe. By understanding what makes humanity function, we are able to define the underlying coding formulated to make a human entity. Doing what humans do best is the process of abiding by the inventor's intensions. Understanding this programming gives us insights into the designer and its motives.

The study of human history is the study of man changing his environment. Humans specialize in change; more specifically, man specializes in the rapid transformation of existence. The rate of manufactured human change in comparison to the rate of evolution is profound. As humanity progresses, change occurs exponentially. Wherever man travels, he will impose this change, transforming landscapes and the form of matter. This course, although perceptually deviant, follows the natural course of the universe as the universe abides by the same design. Humans were designed to impose change at an accelerated pace. This change is in compliance with other components of the universe. Humanity has been provisioned resources to comply with motives of unrelenting change.

Humans have been placed in a scenario that makes change easy to execute. The physical restrictions preventing change are negligible in comparison to human abilities and are only confined by human limitations. The motives ingrained into humanity that perpetuate change have been passed down from the inventor's motives. Change at an accelerated pace, unlike that found in the universe, was a motive imposed onto humanity. Human programming relentlessly wills humanity to propagate change to the greatest extent. The rapidity of this change in relation to other components within the universe is overwhelming. The reasoning behind this rapid change defines the inventor's motives.

A change from one state to another has profound implications. ☐┤╫╢ Things require a change when there is a deficiency or fault in the current state. The universe requires change from its present state. A motive exists in the universe to transform itself into an ideal state that is different from its current condition. This motive has dictated the conditions of all components within the universe; this motive is embedded in the fabric of existence and is subtly transposed into physical things. The urgency driving this motive is profound and has led to the creation of humanity. Humanity unknowingly bears this rooted motive, thereby following an underlying code set by an urgent messenger. This motive has resulted in a creature with many facets and abilities. Humanity is the result of this desire. Humanity is the evidence of the universe's motive.

The Function that Defines the Species

The purpose of the human race is often characterized through the examination of motives imposed onto man by nature. This reasoning concludes that man's constant pursuits should naturally represent the objective of humanity. Humans often associate love with the meaning of life and procreation as being humanity's ultimate goal. The desire to procreate is unavoidable, but this simple feat of survival is a misleading endeavor for such complicated creatures.

Earthly creatures possess an array of traits that define their purpose and function. Each creature attains unique attributes that separate it and its function from other entities. These unique attributes define the purpose of the creature and its function in relation to everything else. □─╫ Each entity is defined by its primary function, which is unique among all other entities. Each creature maintains several secondary functions, but only one unique primary function defines its primary purpose. Other than the primary function, the underlying secondary functions categorize the species abroad. These secondary attributes are common among species with similar characteristics and are often associated as a means to the creature's survival. Some of the common attributes shared among creatures are emotions, procreation, and so on. These features are subservient functions and do not define an entity's purpose.

Any attributes in association with humans and other planetary creatures are not attributes that define humanity's primary function. The attribute that defines humanity is unique and unlike any other trait possessed by any other creature. Humanity's function in relation to all things is extraordinary and categorically foreign to the functions of other creatures. Reducing humanity's function to that of another creature on Earth would place humanity on par with creatures that exist simply for survival. In this scenario, humanity would be slung back to the "caveman era," where procreation was the only insurance for the survival of the species. The urge to multiply is an attribute ingrained in all living entities. Devices put in place to perform this primordial function do not define an entity's purpose. Survival is not by choice but rather is imposed, similar to breathing. An emotional void has been transposed upon humanity that ensures the survival of the species through procreation. The desire to fulfill this need is programmed precisely to the nth degree to ensure the development of the species in support of its primary purpose.

The function that defines the creature and its purpose is distinguished from all other attributes associated with the creature. Each creature possesses a hierarchy of functions, a pyramid of duties, with his or her defining function fixed at the top. Other subservient functions assist in the success of the primary function. Subservient functions are common among all species, but the primary function is unique to a single species. Creatures possess several subservient functions that ensure the primary function succeeds. Although there may be multiple subservient functions present in order to accommodate the primary function, there is only one primary function that requires fulfillment. The primary function is a necessity designed for the fluent operation of nature and, ultimately, the universe. This primary function is a critical operation that must succeed in order for the mechanism of existence to perform. As all things have a purpose in a purposeful universe, they are of a unique and critical function.

The Function of Humanity

A carpenter will use several tools to construct a house. Each tool has a specialized function, and every tool has been refined over time to perform optimally. If the carpenter is faced with a construction obstacle, he acquires a new tool to overcome it, adding the new tool to his arsenal. There is a tool for every trade, and so too the universe produces devices to accomplish every feat. ☐⊢╫ Man is a tool, a device designed for a specific task. Humanity has been created for a purpose and has been granted specific abilities to solve an inherited conundrum. The design of humanity is constantly being refined and improved over previous designs in order to develop an optimal tool for a single purpose.

If I were to hand you a tool that you had never seen or used before, how would you know its purpose? Your investigation would begin like this: first, you would describe the tool's features and compare it to other tools with similar functions. Second, you would attempt to operate the tool on something to see what it can do. Last, you would apply reasoning to its function and deduce how or why someone would use it. Your investigation would follow by examining the application of the tool to discover its function. Discovering humanity's function entails examining what humans do best and which application best suits their abilities. We must match humanity's specialized skills to the most relevant application in the universe. The application humanity has been designed to operate on will reveal the scope and purpose of the tool known as man. The application is the proverbial light at the end of the tunnel that draws humanity toward a fixed goal. The refining of humanity and the accumulation of human potential over time is accredited to the master plan of humanity's destiny. The more we understand humanity's potential, the more clues humans have for discovering what function humanity is architected for and which problems we are designed to solve.

As human skills mature, their designed purpose become more evident, thereby incrementally revealing humanity's ultimate goal. Every stage of human progress reveals evidence toward humanity's ultimate destination. As humans evolve, their design becomes more specialized for the application on which they were meant to operate. Each refinement in the human body provides insight into the task humans were designated to resolve. Humanity's specialized function becomes more distinct from other functions in the universe, isolating the human function from that of other entities. The purpose of humanity materializes as man's specialized function becomes more evident in relation to other functions in the universe. Humanity's function distances itself from other functions, identifying a clear distinction and unique application. Just as all other living creatures serve a function in relation to the Earth, humanity serves a function in relation to its application, existence itself. Features bestowed upon humanity make the human function unique and isolates its purpose from the purpose of other entities. The ability of humans to question their purpose alone places humanity's function in a unique category.

Defining the function of a tool is easier accomplished when the tool is optimized for its purpose. The optimal refinement of a tool mediates its specialized function. Humanity is continually being optimized through the process of progression and evolution. From its initial form, humanity has transformed itself in preparation to fulfill its ultimate obligation. Evolution is a process that yields functional organisms in order to operate in tandem within existence. Changes in habitat cause organisms to evolve quickly in order to sustain life. The human condition has been adapting in a distinct pattern since its conception. The refining of human features has progressed in order to suit a unique application. The transformation of humanity into an optimal tool has continued in one definite direction that leads to a specific application.

Humanity has been developing into a form fit to accommodate its designated duty. For example, consider a purposeful entity whose entire existence relies on moving a boulder from one side of a river to another. After the comprehension of the task is realized, a criterion is formulated to determine the utilities required to complete the task. First, the entity would require a physical body, composed of the same substance of the boulder in order to fluently interact with the object. The physical body must be of ample size and strength to manipulate the boulder. Second, the entity would require tools to move the boulder. It has a thought process that is constantly being refined to give it the opportunity to contemplate a solution. The entity perfects its skills until it can determine a solution. Third, the entity is granted time, and successive entities are produced to fulfill the task if the initial entity is unable to formulate a solution. Successive generations will attempt to supplement the misgivings of the previous generation. Finally, the entity is bestowed with a passion, a yearning for progress. The entity is bestowed with ambitions to complete the task. Actions leading up to the moving of the boulder provide a clear purpose for the entity and its ultimate goal. Similarly, human actions define the purpose of humanity and provide a clear definition for its cause.

The Meaning of Life

The Romans were the first to introduce the dome structure, an intricate design based on weight transfer. Each block of the dome relies on the previous blocks for its support; removing one would compromise the integrity of the entire structure. The universe operates in a similar manner, composed of several devices that rely on each other to maintain the whole. Devices in the universe serve other devices and operate as functions, building a hierarchy that works in unison. Devices atop the hierarchy rely on several lower level devices. These devices are subservient to other devices and support the underlying structure. When we view the universe as a series of functions, we can break it down into simple terms, into a system of devices. One prominent device in the hierarchy is the human race, created for a simple yet critical function. Humans rely on a series of devices in order to exist, as too the universe in turn requires humanity for a specific function in order for it to operate.

Humans are unique creatures with special abilities unlike any other devices in the universe. We have the ability to understand our circumstances and the principles governing them. Our consciousness and minds allow us to contemplate complex thoughts. These abilities single out the human race for a specific function. No other device in the universe operates under similar conditions. The evolution of the human race has forged a foreseeable destiny for humanity. Evidence aggregated from human history paves a distinct path for humanity's purpose. The refinement of the human race has prepared humanity for its ultimate goal.

At one point in time, the universe was not like it is now. The universe has been changing drastically, separating in various directions from its initial whole state. Although the universe may operate in a unified manner, its components are distinct from one another, separated and dispersed. The state of the universe is in disarray; it is a divided country, isolated and remote. This disorder led to the necessity for a tool to restore the universe's stature, a tool with the abilities to traverse obstacles, formulate equations, solve riddles, and resolve the disorder within itself. The universe needs a tool to correct a state that the whole is unable to solve, a unique device able to repair its present condition.

The universe created humanity out of necessity, therein using an evolutionary process based on a requirement for a self-conscious being with profound abilities to solve complex problems. The universe created humanity as a means of restoring it to its initial state. The universe is in peril, detached and dispersed, unable to repair itself. ☐╫ Humanity is a utility created out of necessity by the universe to operate as its surgeon, to discover, solve, and restore the universe. Humanity is an extension of the universe, an appendage optimally designed to be a problem solver. Humans have become the thinkers of the universe, charged with repairing the universe. Every ability bestowed onto humanity is geared toward this purpose. Our abilities will eventually lead us to a prescribed path of monumental purpose, and the quicker we get to that state, the better.

Healers of the Universe

A flower is composed of several small components that cannot be seen with the naked human eye. Each magnification reveals another realm of components joined together to create a single form. The levels of magnification introduce broader insights once incomprehensible by the human mind. Just as a molecule is a component of a flower, a flower is a component of the universe. Components exist within a hierarchy of realms, with one realm supporting the next. This hierarchy of realms forms existence, each containing components that complement others found on higher realms. In the case of the flower, several molecular components congeal to compose a cell, several cells make up a petal, and so on. A continuous chain of reliance is formed with an underlying component supporting every realm.

Humanity is one piece within a realm designed to support the components of a higher plane. The human species is an entity that exists within another component. Humans, in relation to the universe, are similar to the white blood cells found in a body, designed to repair the condition of its host. White blood cells continually flow through the bloodstream and are devoted to repairing and protecting the host against damage and infections. They are the guardians of the greater organism and serve the host in times of crisis. Humanity is a similar subservient device existing in a lower realm. ☐–‖‖ Humanity's purpose is to aid its ailing host by repairing its critical condition. The accumulated efforts of humanity serve a greater purpose in relation to its host. Once humanity ripens, it will methodically set out to perform its duty instinctively. The condition of the universe will gradually improve as humanity spreads its influence. This process will continue until the patient is healed and fully restored.

The numbers of white blood cells in the body ensure success over infections. If a colony of cells should fail to deter an infection, another batch of cells joins the campaign and perseveres. Multiple human societies ensure the success of humanity's ultimate goal, should one society fail. Similar to white cells, the Earth is home to numerous conscious beings to ensure success. If one group should fail to fulfill its duty, another will take its place. Numbers ensure success and reduce the odds of failure. With the conditions of failure being unacceptable, several groups of conscious beings live throughout the Earth, thus increasing the probability of success.

Appendages of the Universe

Humanity was around for thousands of years prior to the invention of the automobile. Initially, the concept of such a mechanism was inconceivable, but after several generations, the need for efficient travel became a necessity, and humanity's capacity to formulate such a design materialized. The maturation of knowledge was integral for building such a complex machine as the automobile. The obstacle of transportation was overcome by humanity's ability to strategize and solve a dilemma. The competence in humanity's ability to solve such an obstacle suitably lay in the maturity of its knowledge. When presented with the obstacle of transportation, man created a fitting solution to the problem in correlation with his maturity level. Humanity will continue to invent fitting solutions when faced with obstacles. Succeeding generations will continue to advance knowledge, thus allowing for more complex resolutions in order to solve exceedingly complicated obstacles.

From humanity's perspective, the universe is an innate and untamed object. It is a lifeless and bleak entity, operating automatically and governed by physical laws. It has no appendages or conscious force, thus the task of moving a star from one place to another is not directly achievable. Impending disturbances within the universe go unresolved, as the universe does not have the appendages or the knowledge to solve its issues. In response to this conundrum and the necessity to dissolve obstacles, the universe created a device to overcome its barriers. The device is composed of certain attributes to allow it to comprehend obstacles and contemplate complex algorithms that the universe itself cannot formulate. The device is provided a consciousness to decipher and comprehend boundless conundrums, an ultimate appendage to follow its bidding and unravel its predicament. ☐─╫ The evolution of the universe has given rise to a creature programmed to do its bidding automatically. This burdened creature is man.

The universe has developed an accommodating environment to nurture the growth of a conscious creature. Provisions of resources are bestowed in order for the creature to develop mechanisms to advance its progress. The universe has supplied the creature with the precise amount of momentum and encouragement it needs to strive and advance to subsequent developmental stages. Much like a parent, the universe places the creature in the most fruitful location possible in order to stimulate growth and to fulfill its designed intensions. All of these elements have been cultivated with a precise mixture in order to attain the best results. Humanity is the universe's appendage, designed to solve the ultimate obstacle of the universe. The universe has created a proverbial arm to move the stars and adjust space. The universe now possesses sustained knowledge and a databank to preserve this knowledge. The universe now has a consciousness and the ability to decide its future. The universe can now gaze at its glory in bewilderment as it sets out on a journey of self-discovery.

What It Is To Be Human

The human mind is a unique device that categorizes humanity as a complex creature. Unlike other creatures, humans are distinguished by their ability to think and develop fluent thoughts. Humans, as inquisitive creatures, have a desire to solve mysteries in order to satisfy cravings instilled in their minds. The underutilized mind has a constant yearning for more knowledge; this manifests itself in enduring curiosity. Human curiosity has led to the invention of knowledge. To solve daunting questions about existence, humans use a library of knowledge derived from the human experience. Knowledge is humanity's greatest invention, and it was destined to be invented because humans are proficient in collecting experiences. □─┼┼┼ Humans excel at gathering information, processing it, and regurgitating it. This ability alone defines what it is to be human.

Knowledge opens doors to opportunities for exploration, examination, and study. The products developed as a result of knowledge have distinguished humanity from all other creatures. This power places humanity on a higher echelon in the universe and defines a specific function for humanity. Knowledge not only describes what humans are about, it is simply what humans are. Without it, we are not human. As knowledge accumulates alongside human progress, the role that humanity plays in the universe becomes more evident.

The products of human creation have defined humanity. Everything in existence has a purpose, even humans, and visualizing humanity in a general context assists in defining mankind. Nature has bestowed upon us an adventurous spirit that wills humanity to explore the boundaries of existence. Humans are roaming creatures, meant to explore, discover, and develop. Nature has created circumstances that regulate human intuition and the desire to explore, as humans develop in a progressive inclination.

The human condition is carefully regulated. If humans huddle in overpopulated masses, sickness and death ensue. If humans become isolated from social experiences, the mind ceases to function properly, leading to the deterioration of reasoning. Humanity is trapped in an elaborate quandary, conditioned to prepare the species for its ultimate responsibility. An extravagant maze has been constructed, leading humanity down an inevitable path willed by nature. This unconscious force guiding humanity is the fundamental programming contained in the human species.

The Earth is a test bed, a stepping-stone designed to prepare humanity for its ultimate goal. Humanity is constantly being conditioned in preparation for its duties in the universe. It is the test of humanity to progress forward and use its crafted abilities to venture down a path toward its ultimate goal. All human instincts serve this purpose and are designed to assist with humanity's progress. A natural path has been forged for humanity, which deters those who oppose it. This scripted path aligns humanity through a gauntlet of development that leads to an inevitable destination. When humanity neglects this will, it is systematically punished; but when it complies, it is rewarded. The desire to follow this path is invisible, yet also unavoidable.

The human construction is perfectly equipped to handle one mission efficiently. Humans are rapidly evolving creatures designed for the purpose of discovering problems and resolving them. Humans are the healers of the universe and were created by the universe for this very task. Our ingrained will urges us to develop our intellectual abilities and build our skills until we are able to solve the ultimate riddle. Humans are the thinkers of the universe, uniquely equipped to resolve the universe's predicaments. A distressful incident has produced the necessity for a problem solving entity with unlimited potential. The universe's final attempt to resolve its conundrum has introduced a multifaceted creature able to mitigate existence itself.

Change Leads to Fulfillment

Wholeness is defined as containing all elements; belonging properly; exhibiting completeness, self-reliance, and independence. The universe is an evolving entity that relies on several components in order to function, similar to a clock turning with several gears; one gear relies upon another to produce precise changes in sequence. Relationships between components are critical, as the universe requires the interaction of several components in order to function. Relationships between components can be traced back to the finest elements in existence. Equally so, humans rely on several physical and mental supplements in order to survive. These relationships fill a void, a missing component, in an attempt to make a human function. The strife associated with attaining the perfect balance of these components is a constant endeavor. We are driven by desires and emotions to attain fulfillments, to which all humans are susceptible. So long as humans continue to develop, their attempts to achieve these fulfillments will never subside.

Motion gives rise to change. Change is required to enable the process of creation to produce something better, something reformed. The purpose of change is to allow for the improvement of a previous state. Change entails several requirements, one of which is movement from one condition to another. There is a purpose behind the transformation of components changing from one physical state to another, and this purpose is incased within the fundamental coding of the universe. Change is required to improve on a condition. Momentous changes occur to improve on previous conditions, with each successive condition better than the last. Each successive change of a component holds the potential to ultimately improve upon the initial condition. Therefore, the current condition is of the least desirable state, and every successive condition is potentially the most optimal state. This logic follows that change is ultimately for the better. □┤┼┤ In this universe, chickens do not cross roads unless it is to improve their condition.

A change is required when the current state is neither complete nor ideal. A need manifests itself to fulfill this requirement. The process of change is ingrained into the fabric of the universe and everything that exists within it; there is a persistent struggle for elements to attain another state. Until this process of change is vanquished, a state of absolute fulfillment cannot be attained. Only when everything is absolute, fixed, and unchanging will the void be repaired, thereby allowing conclusive fulfillment to be achieved.

> *"I see many people die because they judge that life is not worth living. I see others paradoxically get in killed for the ideas or illusions that give them a reason for living (what is called a reason for living is also an excellent reason for dying). I therefore conclude that the meaning of life is the most urgent of questions."*
>
> Albert Camus (1913 - 1960), The Myth of Sisyphus

Human Aggression

Humans accommodate a spectrum of emotions that influence their actions. Some emotions are more prevalent than others, such as aggression. Aggression is the relentless desire to pursue an ambition. It is often associated with man's desire to dominate his species with the use of force.

Social perceptions of aggression have changed throughout history. Aggressive behavior is currently perceived as a primitive reaction and is shunned by modern societies. Although suppressed, aggression plays a vital role in the makeup of human behavior. Nature has bestowed this tenacious emotion upon humanity to manipulate the rate of human progress. Ambition is at the root of human progress. Complacency within humanity delays human progress and derails it from its natural progressive path. Humanity cannot survive in a state of sustained complacency, so a degree of aggression is injected to generate ambition and friction.

Human aggression is a delicate emotion that is responsible for not only prolific accomplishments but also devastating consequences.

The amount of aggression instilled in a person is precisely balanced to limit their potential consequences. There is a midpoint between the aggressive emotional extremes that manifests into a baseline for human behavior. These levels of aggression are precisely balanced, restraining man from prolonged exposure to extreme emotions. These restraints prevent a human from prolonged aggressive behavior and from becoming extensively complacent. If humanity were to veer away from this precise balance, the world's social order would deteriorate. If the majority of the population was consistently aggressive, humanity would be consumed by conflict. Conversely, if the aggression levels were consistently low, humanity would dwindle and fade into obscurity due to prolonged complacency.

Figure 7 shows the relationship of humanity's progress in relation to its amplitude of aggression. Point B complies with a low rate of progress. It also complies with high levels of complacency (Point B2) and low aggression (Point B1), representing a period of social refinement. Periods of extreme complacency are faced with the opportunity for high aggression (Point P). At Point B, human progression slows to a standstill, placing the species at risk of failing. Point C complies with a stable state of progress, portraying an equilibrium between aggression and complacency (Point C1), bringing the rate of human progress to an average pace. Progress is at its highest position at Point D, where aggression is high (Point D2) and complacency is low (Point D1).

A scenario of high aggression would equate to circumstances consisting of war where societies converge and combine initiatives for a united cause. A high rate of aggression cannot be sustained and ultimately leads to the destabilization of the species. High aggression is the catalyst that contributes to leaps in human progress, as history has shown that the majority of human conflicts have led to achievements in technology and advancements in civilizations. ▢—╫ The natural course of human destruction and rebirth is a calculated component regulating the rate of humanity's progress. The greater the amplitude of aggression a population will exhibit, the less complacent it becomes, inducing change and in the process promoting progress.

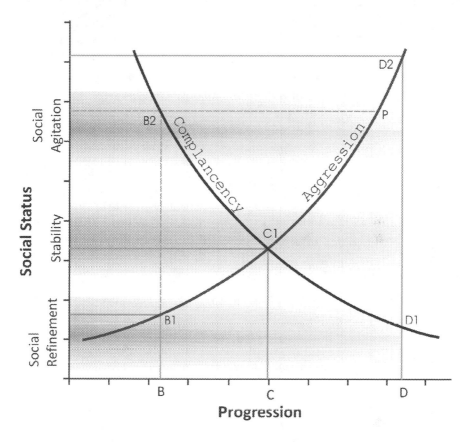

Figure 7   Human Aggression

B - High complacency, low aggression
C - Equal complacency and aggression
D - High aggression and low complacency

Complacency and Growth

Try stopping a ball from spinning in a bucket of swirling water. The ball moves with its medium, the swirling water. Humans are constantly moving within their medium and with the momentum of the universe. Human aspirations fluctuate in peaks and valleys. After achieving an accomplishment, there is a natural tendency to retreat and become complacent. Human complacency comes in varying degrees by design. It is a period of regeneration from expended energy, a period of rest and withdrawal from change. The human condition allows for this state of regeneration to be abused. If influences do not motivate an individual to achieve, the individual will enter into an extended period of complacency. Falling into extended complacency displaces humanity from its momentous medium.

Striving for achievement invokes motives that induce individuals to make a change. An individual's attention span is a mechanism that initiates motives to produce a change. Human attention spans differ between individuals and fluctuate between age groups. The levels of curiosity shared among younger groups are generally higher than among those who have retained more experiences. These levels of curiosity are examples of the methodical ingredients instilled in man to induce change. The precise amount of motivational stimuli keeps mankind in a progressive state.

Humanity is attuned to a specific degree of complacency that cannot be fully realized. Eternal rest is granted only when all the work has been completed. If absolute complacency were realized, then humanity would have reached its progressive end and its peak developmental capacity. If a continual period of rest would ensue, then a return to an Eden-like state would arise. The human species would refrain from production, but continue to consume, and this stagnation would quickly turn into a depletion of resources. The mind-set of humanity would deteriorate, thereby reducing human progress. Humanity's potential for achieving its ultimate goal would evaporate as the amount of change gradually diminished. Humanity would wither away in a sea of universal change.

Humanity is agitated, constantly moving, and progressive. Human attention spans are limited, which keeps us in tune with the nature of existence. Complacency is a limited state, as a person cannot stay complacent when living in a universe of constant change. Whenever extended complacency sets in, the ever-changing nature of existence produces conditions that induce change. Man, as a component of the universe, is willed to inflict change upon its species and its surrounding environment. Positive Opportunism combined with evolution is the process of constantly refining existence in order to avoid extinction. ☐╂╫ Just as matter in the universe is subject to constant change, so too is the human species in the medium of existence. The mind-set of humanity is in tune with this process and continues to follow the natural path of change. Humanity being a component of the universe follows the underlying motives that are instilled into all things. Humanity is part of a process within existence and contains the same motives of change equal to other processes within the universe.

Random and Attractive Events

Boredom and depression are human qualities that influence judgment. Human boredom is a mechanism aimed to draw attention away from an event, triggering a reaction within the subject to move his or her attention to another event. It is a selective process wherein the mind dictates where a human should pay attention and ultimately expend his or her efforts. If humans are wasting their time on unattractive events, the mind alters motives and behaviors to move the subject onto more enticing affairs. Frequent transitions from one event to another are vital for human development. We do not remain transfixed on one event; therefore, we are constantly exploring new horizons and gaining new experiences. Boredom, among other conditions, alters our motives and prevents us from becoming transfixed. Instinctive impulses persuade individuals to pursue other activities by creating attention deficits.

Humans become bored by repetitious activities no matter how engaging the event. The more random the event transpiring, the more interest is sparked and the more appealing the event will be to an individual. The search for new experiences is endless; it feeds our curiosity to discover and explore. We are driven to accumulate new experiences because these events create unique opportunities. Unique experiences, in turn, assist in the invention of creative ideas. Humans, by nature, are inventive creatures and require the accumulation of unique experiences to fuel their inquisitive minds. The more active the mind is, the more desire is instilled within a subject to explore. Inquisitiveness reveals an active mind, as the mind wills the individual to acquire unique experiences in order to develop creative thoughts.

Randomness is appealing; therefore, we purposefully seek unique experiences in hopes of experiencing something new. Humanity is caught in a perpetual circle of enticement and discovery. The motivation to seek out random experiences maintains humanity's ability to invent new technologies and assist in the development of knowledge. The larger the pool of unique experiences that is maintained, the greater the ability to draw upon this knowledge in order to invent unique thoughts. Knowledge is derived from experiencing and recording the methodologies of the physical world. The expansion of experiences through technology ensures greater knowledge. Man's relentless curiosity has kept the species progressing. This motivating mechanism has improved over time, bringing humanity closer in line with its purpose.

Consider the mixing of primary colors as an example of random experiences. Two primary colors, when combined, create a new color. Mixing the newly created colors with another primary color creates yet another color. The mixing of colors can continue indefinitely, continually expanding the color possibilities. Figure 8 depicts the magnitude of color possibilities when mixing three primary colors from Column B. The mixing of the primary colors expands to several alternative colors in Column F, similar to the accumulation of experiences that lead to the discovery of new knowledge. The more experiences you possess, the more creative thoughts you can conjure. Humanity's ability to transform new experiences into knowledge is an integral component of human progress. The uniqueness of this newfound knowledge is dependent upon the library of prior knowledge. ☐─╫╫ Boredom is a human mechanism designed to attune humanity's focus on prevalent things in order to facilitate the acquisition of new knowledge. Greater human curiosity and inquisitiveness results in a higher rate of knowledge acquisition.

Figure 8　　　　Diversity of Events and Colors

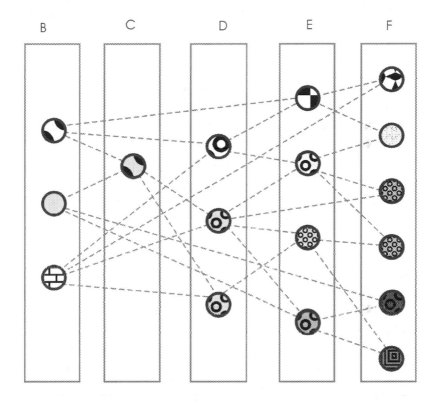

B - 7 color possibilities
C - 64 aggregate possibilities
D - 1176 aggregate possibilities
E - 397802 aggregate possibilities
F - 54992287451 aggregate possibilities

Experiencing new events contributes to the expansion of knowledge. As societies advance, the opportunity to attain unique experiences increase. Globalization assists in the process of pooling knowledge and broadening experiences. Knowledge is humanity's niche, and its attainment is the key to humanity's success over its ultimate goal. The mind will continue to entice the individual to seek out unique experiences. Seeking knowledge becomes a pleasurable activity, making human progress motivationally enticing. The more enticing it is to attain knowledge, the more rapidly humanity will provision itself for its ultimate goal.

The Stepping-Stones of Discovery

Humans learn about the physical world in stages, placed in a sequence of steps, one grander than the last. Each step is like a stone protruding out of a river, where each stone is positioned a little farther away than the last. In order to reach the next stone, one must jump farther and farther. Crossing the river requires practice jumping on the first two stones until the skill of jumping farther builds. The steps involved in human development fall into a precise mold, similar to that of any developing creature. ☐┤╢ The progress of human development adheres to a logical process that systematically builds the species' knowledge. This process has been refined over time but consistently follows an evident path designed for the human race. Humanity experiences the results for the passing of stages as a product of human achievement, although the process in reality is an invisible routine formulated for the human condition. Humans, like other entities, follow this invisible routine unknowingly. This automatic process of development paints a clear destination of successive stages, leading to humanity's ultimate end.

Humans acquire skills through sequential stages of life. Children go through the educational system in incremental stages. The completion of certain stages advances a child on to higher levels of education. Each level of skills training they attain is limited to the learning capacity that an average human can absorb at a given age.

The degree of skill setting increases during each successive stage in proportion to a predefined criteria. The educational system prepares pupils in successive stages so that they will be adjusted for the sequential stages they will encounter. Human progress as a whole operates in a similar fashion. The development of humanity from its initial state to the present has progressed in a proportional fashion. These proportional segmentations are mitigated by the experiential exposure exhibited by the human species. Humanity gains experience by interacting with the physical world and mastering environments. Once humans master their immediate environment, they move onto other environments in an attempt to master them. The environment represents the classroom in this scenario, and graduating to successive stages requires mastery of the present classroom. Each environment that is mastered is a completion of a stage, during which humanity has attained the skill set required to move on to other environments.

The completion of stages is the process of attaining knowledge. As knowledge accumulates, opportunities for new discoveries arise. Each environment mimics a microcosm of the next, building upon the already attained skill set acquired during the previous stages. Reaching sequential stages requires a level of skill that can only be acquired by mastering the present environment. This process hinders the attainment of top-level stages prior to the acquisition of lower-level stages. The process amalgamates into a stepping-stone schema wherein each subsequent level is proportionally grander than the last and lies just beyond the pupil's abilities. Traversing each stepping-stone requires a little more knowledge and development than the last. The obstacles in each stage are the training grounds required to challenge humans in order to develop their skills and to progress to sequential stages.

The magnitude of each stage is proportionate to the ratio of human development and the human capacity to learn. This design of gradual discovery consists of the building blocks required for humanity to develop into its ultimate potential. Humanity acquires knowledge of the world in concise doses, a process that limits its exposure to experiences that are far above the learning curve. Experiences beyond human contemplation are reserved for future stages of development. For instance, things that humans are not supposed see are not revealed until the time is right. This gradual course of discovery prepares humanity for future endeavors. As technology advances, windows begin to open that reveal new staging grounds of learning for the next subsequent stages of development.

Social Control and Aggression

Aggression can be perceived as a positive or negative attribute, depending on its application. Aggression lends itself to agitation, a change from the present. Change is a positive attribute in association with human progress, thus an appropriate amount of aggression is beneficial for humanity. Aggressive societies have advantages over passive societies. They generally advance quicker socially and technologically. These advancements determine the likelihood of the society's survival, thus the promotion of aggression is encouraged. When aggression is abused, negligible events tend to follow in quick succession. Successes reaped from aggression ultimately lead to the demise of a society. Societies that practice aggression often become overly aggressive and falter. Excessive aggression leads societies to implode, a state that leads to instability and chaos. The negative aspect of progressive aggression is that the society practicing it will eventually collapse; therefore, controls must be put in place to mitigate aggression and restrict it to an optimal level. An ideal society controls aggression at a level that promotes competitive progress while deterring social implosion. ☐⊢╫ The task of maintaining societal prosperity depends on the ability of governing agents to optimally manipulate aggression controls. Greater countermeasures must be deployed in societies that exhibit higher rates of aggression. The higher the rate of aggression, the more social controls the society must impose. An aggressive society must also enforce greater penalties and repercussions for aggressive behavior. Aggressive societies are suppressed by laws that restrict aggressive behavior.

The prosperity of a society lies in the balance of promoting and restricting aggression with regulations. Figure 9 illustrates the relationship between social aggression and control. The greater the aggressive curve exuded by a society, the more social controls must be employed by governing agents to stabilize societal cohesion. Without these restrictions, a society is susceptible to chaos and a breakdown in its social order. Societies A, B, and C have different levels of aggression. Society A is subjected to the maximum amount of restrictions and has been designated as an aggressive state, whereas Society C has a minimal aggression slope and has been designated as a

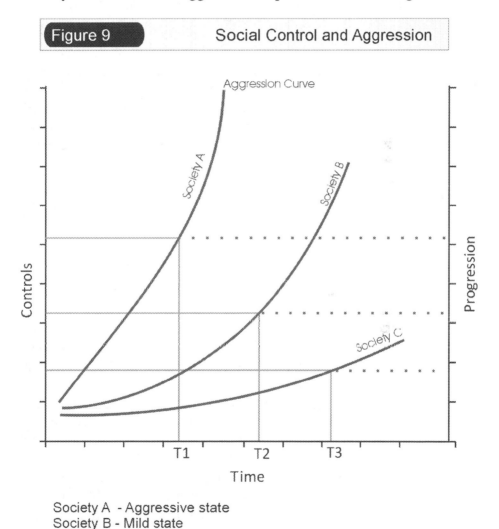

Figure 9   Social Control and Aggression

Society A - Aggressive state
Society B - Mild state
Society C - Passive state
Aggression Curve ————————

passive society. At any given time (Point T), the governing state must deploy the appropriate controls to counterbalance the degree of aggression. Society A has the opportunity to attain a higher level of progress, but these achievements result in tighter controls, restricting the society. Without proper social controls, Society A will inevitably implode into its aggressive behavior.

The Separation of Man from the Physical World

There are two pronounced states of man: the physical and the mental. The manipulation of the human condition through evolution has enhanced the physical human body. The brain being of physical substance has evolved as well, creating an efficient memory storage device with the capacity to generate elaborate thoughts. The later stages of humanity's progression are interlinked with humanity's ability to master the body with the mind. As human intelligence continues to increase, the realm of thought will transcend the physical world. Just as humanity has transcended through stages of physical development, it will inevitably enter an era of mental prowess, a state in which the physical world has been shed for mental aptitudes to rule.

The physical and mental realms have unique characteristics because they exist on separate plateaus. □┼╫ Humanity's progress includes mastering the thought realm, thereby dissolving the facade of the physical world. Reaching this objective creates a deepening separation between the physical and mental realms. In order to master the mental realm, a degree of separation between the physical and mental worlds is required. Physical influences on the body affecting the mind must be subdued. Experiences that stimulate the five senses should be contained and controlled. Reality becomes a subject of thought and a separate entity dictated by logical conditions. The physical realm dissolves into figments of the mind's contemplation as reality is controlled and understood through thought. The further humanity disassociates itself from the physical world, the more it strives toward the successive levels of progression. The physical world becomes an inanimate condition, subject to the laws of physical principles. Existence becomes a science experiment understood through the eyes of logic.

Humanity's connection to the physical world rests in a domineering position, as our senses are exposed to the physical world our entire lives. Although logical thought has progressed through science, the true mastery of the mind's realm occurs when existence is entirely defined through the use of principles. Physical laws predicting the nature of matter have become exceedingly reliable, but there are too many unknowns to define the actions of matter indefinitely. Although logical reasoning has placed a permanent footprint upon the causes of events within the material world, the abundant amount of unknowns has reserved the task of defining the physical world by means of experiment.

Humanity is susceptible to the physical world, no matter how much logic is applied to the quantification of events. Physical influences make humans react, thereby negating logical reasoning. For instance, an itch is a cause for a scratch; a scream is an instinctive reaction when someone is scared. The more we rely upon these instinctive reactions, the less we are in tune with logical thought. Human immaturity is displayed when it succumbs to physical influences. Primordial instinctive reactions, which have assisted in human survival, continue to influence human judgment and impede human progress. These influences have become useless appendages, a cancer weighing down on the progress of humanity. Evolution's inability to keep pace with human progress has created a hindrance that can only be remedied through human ingenuity. Physical awareness was a necessity in the absence of logic, but as logical reasoning gains momentum, humanity should perceive physical influences as a subject of science. Relinquishing these physical influences is another phase of humanity's progress. The more humanity succumbs to these primordial influences, the more it hinders its growth.

Secrets of the Mind

"You should pray for a sound mind in a sound body."

Juvenal (55 AD - 127 AD), Satires

The Mind's Potential

Muscles require energy in order to operate, and the more energy supplied to the muscle, the greater the production. The brain is similar to a muscle that utilizes a vast amount of the body's energy. The more the brain is utilized, the larger it gets, thereby requiring more energy. Picture this scenario: several light bulbs are connected together under a single circuit that is connected to a battery, as shown in Figure 10. When the battery power is released, the voltage is divided equally among all the bulbs, which shine at equal luminosity. If you remove some of the bulbs, the remaining bulbs become brighter. As we remove each light bulb, we find that the remaining bulbs get brighter and brighter until the final bulb burns the brightest. The brain works in a similar fashion. The brain has several utilities plugged into it, draining it of its resources. The five senses are in constant interaction with the brain and demand most of its processing power. When all the senses are operating at equal potential, the brain becomes overutilized, thereby trying to focus on sensorial operations rather than logical reasoning. In this scenario, none of the senses can operate at their full potential as the brain reserves processing resources equally to all amenities. In the end, the processing resources reserved for each sense becomes diluted. Every sense becomes less inquisitive and runs under less power as the brain divides its resources. If for instance you were to remove one of the senses, the others become stronger in their ability and resourcefulness. For example, a blind man might develop a more powerful sense of touch, which compensates for his loss of sight, or a deaf person might develop a greater sense of smell with the absence of hearing.

Figure 10 Luminescent bulbs

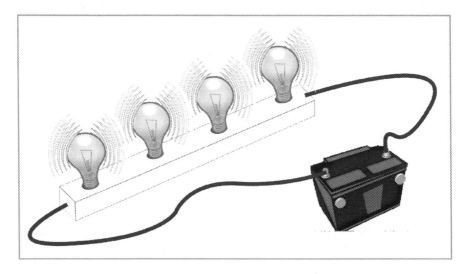

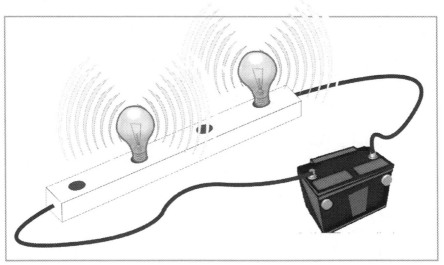

Utilities tapping the brain's processing power limit the full potential of each utility. We tend to use concentration and focus to funnel the brain's resources toward one selective task. For example, we close our eyes to focus on hearing, or we insulate ourselves from distractions in order to focus on studying. When focusing intellectual power on one task, other mundane activities will draw less brainpower. The physical body is constantly utilizing the brain's resources to such an extent that the mind can never be fully focused on a single function. When focusing, we can only attempt to reach the full potential of our brain's thinking capacity. □⊢╫ The full potential of the brain resides in the attainment of pure thought, a state that utilizes the mind's resources for thoughts alone. By reducing the amount of utilities tapping the brain's resources, we can attempt to achieve pure thought. We achieve this state by eliminating physical influences and distractions that interact with human senses. We cannot completely eliminate our senses because we would no longer be labeled human if we did. So we can only come close to achieving pure thought, yet never realize it.

Our ability to utilize the brain's optimal capacity allows for the improvement of the mind's proficiency. The process of utilizing the brain's optimal performance is a vital aspect toward humanity reaching its ultimate goal. This mental state introduces the process of heightened thinking and the ability to think greater thoughts more fluently. Meditation is one method of eliminating sensory perception and focusing on thought. Many insights have come from meditation. Practicing meditation trains the mind to focus on thoughts, but the process only works in tranquil areas where concentrating on thoughts is effortless. Humans are social creatures that cannot sustain a prolonged meditative state, as the urge for physical experiences overwhelms us. Further, the human body cannot sustain sensory deprivation for extended periods of time. Attaining the conditions of optimal thought is the technique of reaching humanly limits and then releasing the pursuit to ease mental strain. People exercise thought by processing stored experiences they have gathered from the physical world. These experiences are databanks of information used to create unique thoughts. The ideal condition for achieving pure thought lies in the balance of attaining worldly experiences and then processing them with meditation.

The Conformity of the Mind

Evolution and time share a common bond; as time progresses, things inevitably change. Change introduces complexities into the universe that require conforming, while evolution attempts to mitigate that change through conformity. Evolution entails a process that allows matter to adapt. Change can be progressive or regressive; evolution is the process involved with the positive aspect of changing matter. Conforming matter to a specific circumstance ensures a greater chance of survival. Matter has been programmed to conform in order to adapt to changing circumstances; equally so, humans adapt to circumstances in order to remain relevant. The mind is instinctively programmed to conform to outside influences. The mind is susceptible to external influences that dominate the host's surrounding environment. People change the way they think, talk, and look to conform to their surroundings. Conforming to one's environment is an elementary evolutionary process that ensures a greater chance of survival. If you successfully adapt to your environment, your chances of survival increase.

The practice of elongating body parts involves abusing parts of the body over time, thereby manipulating their shape. The mind, too, takes time and momentum to permanently adapt to external influences. The mind is a device that takes shape based on exposure to external influences. If the mind is exposed to constant and consistent deviant behavior, it will adapt to that behavior. Predominant experiences are those that shape the mind's thinking patterns. If you can control and manipulate experiences absorbed by the mind, you can change thought processes. Controlling a mind involves controlling the experiences the mind is absorbing. Constant exposure to a consistent experience will force the mind to adapt to those projected experiences.

The mind is constantly active and being utilized by the body to process sensorial experiences. Building a strong mind can be achieved through the practice of logical reasoning. Reality is subjective, and changing one's perception of reality allows for a pliable mind to be manipulated. There are ways to make the mind less pliable and more rigid. □-HH Exercising the mind helps to strengthen perceptions and makes the mind less susceptible to external influences. Conditioning the mind requires focusing on thought and relying on logic rather than reality. Strengthening channels in the mind by focusing intently allows for greater criticism of external influences through reasoning. If subjective reality is constantly questioned through the use of reasoning, perceptions become difficult to manipulate.

Conceptual Filters and Perception

Rain accumulating on a road will gradually form a stream that winds down a path toward a drain. Along the path, the flowing water may encounter obstacles that divert the stream before it reaches its destination. The water flows along the path of least resistance as it courses around larger obstacles and through minuscule ones. Human thought processes operate in a similar manner. There is a series of procedures involved in the construction of thought. A thought traverses a conduit of experiential filters, which manipulate the thought's initial denotation. Filters derive from experiences ingrained in the mind and stored as memories. Experiences manipulate and affect the mind by creating filters in memory through which thoughts pass and thereby are influenced. As the mind grows, filters mature and create fixed obstacles that permanently divert the paths of thought flow. The comprehensiveness of the initial thought is lost as it passes through these filters. The ability to comprehend rational thought from the experiential world becomes distorted as mental filters obscure reality.

Thoughts travel through mind filters, which manipulate, deter, or transform their initial properties. Predominant filters derived from lasting influential experiences sway thoughts with prejudice. The more extreme the influential experience, the greater the manipulative effect it will pose upon the thought processing conduits. For example, if a person flips a coin that lands on heads every time (with probable logic dismissed), he would logically come to believe that heads is the only possible outcome. The repetitive experience of the coin flip creates a prejudice filter and forces the mind to produce a conclusive belief regarding the future outcomes of coin flips. Until the individual experiences an instance where the coin lands on tails, his mind will continue to make the same prediction for future results. Figure 11 shows the relationship between thought flow and filters. The initial instance of the thought (B) is derived from an experience. The thought (B) traverses through conduits (C) and collides with several experiential filters (D-F). Some of the components of the thought are then blocked (E) or redirected (F) prior to reaching the output of the individual's perceived reality (H). Other components flowing through experiential filters (M) transform their initial attributes by manipulating the context of the thought.

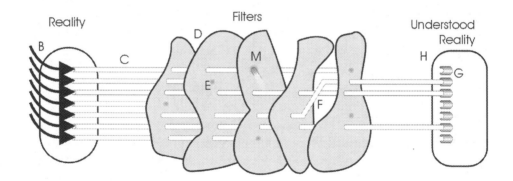

Figure 11   Filters of Thought

B - Initial thought
C - Thought conduit
D - Experiential filters
E - Blocked process
F - Shortest path, redirected conduit
G - Output medium
H - Thought output
M - Manipulated thought

Experiences of monumental influence create dominant filters that drastically control thought processes. Thoughts follow the path of least resistance. Dominant filters harden thought conduits, forcing them to flow along a certain path. Repetitive experiences harden filters in the mind, thereby creating a new perceived reality. A mature individual's mind contains hardened filters that manipulate thoughts so much so that they become accustomed to flowing through certain avenues. Thoughts blocked by filters find the next accessible conduit through which to flow in order to complete their journey. If a conduit is obscured by a filter, the thought finds the least resistant conduit to flow through. Thoughts flow down the path of minimal energy expenditure unless the individual forcibly changes the thought's direction by means of concentration. The process of thought flowing down paths with least resistance insures energy conservation, thereby reserving energy for times of deep thought. Instinctive thoughts require no reasoning and therefore will not utilize precious energy from the mind.

Each individual perceives reality in a unique light, as each person accumulates unique experiences. No two individuals share the same lifelong experiences; therefore, everyone contains unique thought patterns. ⬜╟┤ Every person has unique filters that affect how their thoughts are processed. Reality is perceived uniquely as perceptions vary from person to person. Enclosed societies retain an underlying common perception shared among citizens as they are exposed to similar experiences. A general commonality of thought patterns are adopted among people with similar experiences. Populations living in close proximity begin to think alike as they are exposed to the same mediums. Perceptions become similar when individuals share similar experiences. The closer two individuals are to each other, the more streamlined their perceptions and thought filters. Swaying the masses becomes a systematic process as the unconsciousness inherits similar biases.

There are methods for desanitizing imbedded filters, thereby changing an individual's perception. The initial steps of desanitization require identifying existing filters, including dominant filters. The primary filters that obscure thought and warp reality are those experiences that have inflicted the greatest influences. To negate these experiences, one must introduce stronger influential experiences, thereby creating venues that bypass existing filters. Convincing someone who has experienced only the outcome of heads in a coin flip that the next flip will be tails will require several experiential instances where the coin lands on tails. Alternatively, the person can be exposed to the ideas of probability and odds, thus undermining the experiences and erasing the belief that a coin can only land on one side.

How Great Thinkers Think

Attaining the optimal performance from the brain requires degrees of mind conditioning and concentration. The brain is an interactive device; therefore, getting the most out of the device depends on how one uses it. The brain has a capacity to conduct several processes simultaneously. Each process requires a portion of the brain's processing power, thus diminishing the proportional processing power for each individual activity. An activity that the mind is often used for is problem solving, which requires concentration. Concentration entails focusing thoughts on one subject by eliminating thoughts on other subjects. Subjective focus requires eliminating distractions that siphon the brain's processing resources and reserving resources for primary thought.

Those who are distracted by mundane human actions cannot concentrate on deep thought and cannot aspire to great thinking. Great thinkers practice canceling out mundane distractions to keep their mind focused on primary thought. Primary thought is more readily achieved when an individual is isolated and is avoiding sensorial distractions, which tap resources from the mind. By doing this, the mind becomes trained and accustomed to filtering out distractions that absorb resources. The mind develops into a refined tool, one that is able to concentrate on a primary thought while neglecting sensorial experiences. Utilizing the mind for a single purpose instead of many mediocre tasks will yield better results. The constant practice of concentrating conditions the mind to devote its full potential toward one objective.

Training one's mind is vital for great thinking. The mind must be refined in order to allow complex thoughts to be processed fluently. The mind is a tool that can be honed into a specialized device. With repetitive training of focused thought, the mind builds a capacity to accommodate enhanced thinking. ⬜⊣⊩ Similar to the mastery of physical feats with a conditioned body, so, too, the mind builds a tendency to think efficiently through the consistent practice of complex thinking. By exposing the mind to several challenges consistently, the mind builds a callus, an ability to decipher complex challenges with ease. Neural paths within the mind physically increase in number and size to accommodate the increase in electrical activity. The mind becomes a refined muscle able to flex and produce great thoughts fluently.

Controlling Impulses

Differences in behavioral control exist between a child's mind and an adult's mind. Control over the mind's prowess entails restraints over impulses, emotions, and actions. For instance, the ability to repress feelings of anger is a daunting task for an adult, let alone for a child. The ability to control human impulses displays the maturity level of a mind. Humanity's only escape from its primordial urges lies in the progressive maturing of the human mind. The more civil humanity becomes, the less susceptible it is to responding to primal urges. Civil societies promote the suppression of primal urges by imposing social restraints. These social restraints are endorsed by institutions found throughout civil societies. Civil societies are commended for their ability to control human behavior. Civil minds are said to be in compliance with civil statutes when controlling primal urges and suppressing primal thoughts.

The more control an individual has over his behavioral impulses, the greater his ability to suppress primal urges. Mental control is a sign of intelligence, as intelligent minds have the tenacity to analyze thoughts before they are acted upon. Urges such as anger, panic, and sexual impulses are more easily repressed by intelligent individuals. ☐–╫ The more intelligent a person is, the more immune he is toward acting upon primal impulses. Susceptibility to impulses is a cause for impulsive behavior. This type of behavior identifies those who have little control over their minds. The ability to subdue primal urges is the process of keeping the mind conditioned in order to avoid susceptibility to experiential influences. These influences ignite primal urges when thought is directed from logical reasoning. These influences prey upon the human condition and conjure actions based on emotions.

The Pursuit of Achievement

The concept of humanity is similar to an intricate mechanism, a device built for one intention. Humanity, like any enterprise, has a goal and an objective. The attainment of this objective requires humans to pass through a succession of achievements. These tasks are achieved by select groups who specialize in specific abilities. Every achievement requires a uniquely conditioned group that specializes in the practice of its task. ☐–╫ There is a hierarchy of tasks that humanity is designated to accommodate in the attainment of humanity's ultimate goal. If the designated groups are not accomplishing the highest of tasks within the hierarchy, their focus turns to secondary tasks that aid in the achievement of primary tasks. If secondary tasks are not pursued, groups accommodate tertiary tasks in order to assist in the completion of the secondary tasks. If groups are not directly pursuing the ultimate goal for humanity, then they redirect their efforts to other mediocre activities that indirectly assist in the attainment of the ultimate goal.

Human progress and the pursuit of knowledge are the primary measures required for the attainment of humanity's ultimate goal. Any task that varies from these primary tasks reduces humans to accomplishing secondary tasks. Procreation is a potent secondary task that assists in the success of the primary tasks. The need for humans to pursue secondary tasks is far greater than the pursuit of the primary task, as these tasks are more vital and therefore require more participants. Accomplishing humanity's ultimate goal requires intelligence and its pursuit. Those who are actively pursuing intelligence are less motivated to pursue secondary tasks. Those who develop knowledge pursue primary tasks and become substantial contributors to humanity's progress. Knowledge advances mankind, as it is the primary means for attaining humanity's ultimate goal. Those who practice the acquisition of distinguished knowledge are able to restrain their primordial impulses, the ones that promote secondary tasks that are positioned lower on the hierarchy of human achievement. Those who negate the practice of intelligence are, thus, more susceptible to primal motives that support those groups pursuing primary tasks. The success of primary tasks requires substantially more participants in pursuing secondary tasks. Desires to address other tasks that are not primary become inflated, as lower level tasks require more participants. The success of the primary task directly relies on the success of tasks positioned lower on the hierarchy. Therefore, humanity is conditioned to pursue tasks at the bottom of the hierarchy rather than those positioned at the top.

Figure 12 shows the relationship between the practice of intelligence and the pursuit of humanity's goal. The greater the intelligence, the more inclination an individual will have toward pursuing humanity's primary tasks (D). Less intelligence leads to the pursuit of supporting tasks (B), which assist the primary tasks. Like the cohesiveness of a stacked pyramid of cards, each individual pursues a task that supports another. The base of the structure is vital in the support of the cards positioned on top. The base of the structure requires more cards in order to support those cards on top.

| Figure 12 | Pursuit of Tasks |

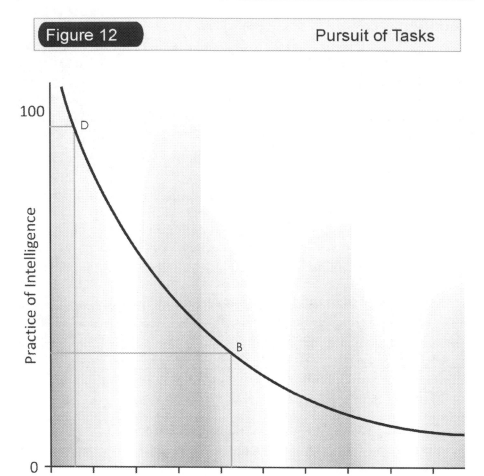

D - High practice of intelligence leads to focus on primary tasks
B - Low practice of intelligence results in pursuit of secondary tasks

Rational and Emotional Thought

A rational person tends not to be swayed by emotions. Emotions bring about biased opinions derived from subjective experiences. Judgments influenced by emotions incorporate interpersonal motives that divert opinions from logical reasoning. Emotions have no context in the realm of science and are perceived as a liability. Emotions are a primitive human attribute that divert thoughts from logical reasoning. As humanity progresses through the technological age, the transition to logical reasoning becomes more prudent. Civil states practice the withdrawal of emotionally driven judgment when abiding by concepts based on reasoning. Rational societies adopt a logical consensus, as they are governed by laws and regulations that adhere to logical principles.

Emotionally driven thought is suppressed within rational societies. Reasoning is the practice of separating emotions from subjective judgments. Although practical, this practice subdues the human condition as humans are prone to emotional decisions. Separating humans from their emotions diminishes the definition of a human. As humans suppress their emotions, they also suppress a vital component required for their existence. Sustaining a withdrawal of emotional thought is unattainable; therefore, humans practice the periodic withdrawal of emotions during periods of focus. Periods of concentration subdue emotions and allow for rational thought to prevail. During periods of emotional release, restrained emotions are exhausted. This cycle of emotional control has become the challenge of modern man; those who have mastered the balance of rationality and emotional thought are suitable for civil societies. Those who can suppress their emotional behavior meet the calling of civil societies.

Emotional expressions are practiced throughout childhood as they arise unconsciously, like a reflex. Emotions are unavoidable and play a vital role in the progress of humanity. Eliminating emotion would go against the coding instilled in humans. Humans are susceptible to irrationality, as emotions guide the majority of human behavior. Rational thought and emotional thought cannot, ultimately, coexist. If a person succumbs to constant emotional behavior, rational thought is unattainable.

The ability to control emotions gives rise to rational thinking. ☐┼╫ The more rational a person is, the less susceptible he or she is to emotional persuasion. Thinking in the best of terms is the process of controlling emotional tendencies. Controlling primitive tendencies exemplifies the mind's ability to master the body. The ability to control emotions reveals a great thinking human and a rationally conditioned mind. Rational minds are able to suppress emotions and exist in serenity. Those who are great thinkers live soundly.

Pure Thought

The universe is an amalgamation of several realms, a conduit allowing for dissimilar constituencies to interact. The universe has rules for the interaction of elements. There is a fundamental parent-to-child relationship between interacting elements, beginning with the founding constituencies that formed the universe. The layered realms in the universe allow for certain elements to interact, but do not allow all elements to interact with one another. This relationship creates a hierarchy of permitted interaction, where elements form a proverbial chain of interaction. This hierarchy allows elements to interact indirectly with one another through the elements found in between.

Matter and fields are different substances that interact within distinct realms. Similarly, thought is an exclusive element that interacts with the physical realm through a medium. In order for thought to interact with the physical universe, a conduit, the mind, is required. The brain is a component of the material realm and acts as a venue, allowing thought to be conveyed into the physical realm. Without these venues, thoughts alone could not interact with the physical world. The body provides the vessel, a tool that allows matter to be manipulated through the development of thoughts.

Everything in the physical world has limitations. Matter itself conflicts with its medium, causing resistance. Substances of matter tend to cause friction when in motion. There is a constant resistance to matter in the physical realm. Fields that use matter as a conduit for the physical realm adopt this resistance. □─╫╢ Being trapped in the physical world limits the mind and its full capacity to produce fluent thought. Physical influences cause thought to waver as the mind becomes regulated by the venue from which it interacts in the physical realm. Energy that was once able to flow without resistance has to slog through matter. This resistance reduces the efficiency of the thought process. Thinking requires more energy to overpower the resistance attributed to matter. The process of thinking becomes a struggle, making concentration reserved for occasions. Concentration becomes a taxing exercise and cannot be sustained for long durations. Thinking exponentially causes the physical condition of the mind to change, resulting in the evaporation of energy. The flow of thought is resisted and can never reach its full potential.

An electronic circuit board processes electrons by manipulating electrical paths to produce specific outputs. Electrons pass through components called *resistors* that limit the amount of electricity passing through the circuit. Without resistors, electricity would flow at an unregulated rate, similar to lightning striking the ground during a thunderstorm. The brain acts like a complicated circuit board with billions of resistors. The resistors prevent the fluent flow of thought as thoughts course through the circuits of the brain. The mind's capacity to think is unlimited, but its ability to process unlimited thoughts is regulated by the principles governing matter. The process of thought flowing through the brain is resisted and is contingent upon its medium. The matter medium keeps thoughts from traversing at unbounded speeds and at limitless capacity. Thoughts become a condition of the physical realm as they are resisted and subject to time, thereby leaving the attainment of pure unrestricted thought by means of releasing thought from its resisting medium.

Randomness

The brain is an electrochemical device that requires several mechanisms working in unison. The predominant functions operating in the brain are memory storage and calculative processing. Memory, or experiential data storage, is mainly made up of archived memory and volatile memory. Archived memory is divided further into precedent and non-precedent memory. These mechanisms work in tandem to develop an efficient thought producing device. The process of evolution has refined these mechanisms so that they work in unison with each other to an efficient degree, making the process of thinking humanity's greatest asset. Humanity has become dependent on fluid thought, and this necessity has been accommodated by evolution. Processes within the mind have evolved to create a device capable of producing thought more fluently.

The brain is a simple input-output device, taking in experiences by way of senses, and then producing output through thought. Inputs are attained through experiences accumulated and stored in memory. The more input provided to the brain, the greater the amount of possible output. The uniqueness of the experiences a person collects determines the possible uniqueness of his or her produced thoughts. ☐┼╫ The variety of memories stored within the mind determines the brain's capacity to contemplate unique outputs. Solving riddles, for instance, is a task best suited for an individual with vast experiences. Utilizing a variety of stored memory allows for better possible conclusions to unique problems. Becoming a profound problem solver entails the acquisition of diverse and ample experiences. Those who wish to find answers must have a desire to acquire extensive experiences. The more the mind is exposed to experiences, the more easily it is able to solve problems.

Solving math equations requires logical analysis, as each equation has a definite answer. In the relative world, the mind attempts to obtain the best answer for each mathematical equation based on stored experiences. The results for the best answer are not a random guess, but rather a calculation, a computational process that inserts variables from events into equations. These mathematical results do not always lead to a definite answer in reality. For instance, if someone were to guess the outcome of a dice roll, they would have a probability of 17 percent, or one chance in six, of being correct. Adding an additional die adds to the complexity of the possible outcomes when determining the possible combined product of the dice. For instance, if the dice are rolled a hundred times and, on average, the product of the rolls is eight, more than any other total based on a hundred rolls, a person would guess that the next roll will add up to the most probable number that has appeared in the previous hundred rolls: eight. An individual would predict the most likely total number to appear would be eight, and this would be the best guess based on his experience. However, mathematical statistics tell us that the probability of the product of the dice roll is likely to be seven, rather than eight. Although experience determines the relative conclusion of the results, mathematical calculations may differ when discussing the likelihood in reality. This situation demonstrates that reality is not always identical to practical science. Science's inability to explain definite results gives rise to the concept of randomness or chance. Therefore, the statistical probability of a likely outcome can only be hypothesized.

Statistics is an accommodating principle for humanity. It allows for a gray area of possibilities and gives credibility to events of chance. Whenever an occurrence, such as the roll of dice occurs, the inability to predict the next roll with precision does not mean the mathematical equations are flawed, but rather the equation explaining the results is inadequate. The results from the experiments have relative variables not taken into consideration, making the equation for the probability of the total sum insufficient. The difference between practical and practice exceeds man's capacity of comprehension. Man simply applies a statistical equation to define a probable outcome, negating other relative variables, which define the results. Understanding the complexities involved in a dice roll go beyond human comprehension; therefore, the human mind calculates odds using statistical probability, even though probability is not adequate for deciphering the definite outcome of a roll. Human experiences are far more complicated than rolls of dice, making each output or conclusion seem random. This creates the illusion of random thoughts derived from nothingness, where in actuality thoughts are a conglomeration of past experiences digested by the mind. The mind bases decisions on stored experiences, and because those experiences appear to be unique, it becomes easy to say that the outcomes of the decisions are random.

Thoughts have one resolute outcome and are unique to each individual, as each individual retains unique information about his or her experiences. The complexity in determining the source of a decision is too vast to comprehend; this as a result creates the conclusion that thoughts are random. In actuality, thoughts derived from the mind are amalgamations of stored experiences that fill in the pieces of a prescribed output. A process in the mind conjures new thoughts by recycling stored memory, piecing bits together, providing a definite output. Uniqueness is only found in the combination of unique experiences used to piece together the thought. Uniqueness is more prevalent when the mind has more experiences to apply to when amalgamating a thought. Obtaining more experiences broadens the mind and its capacity to produce unique thoughts. Equally so, it strengthens the illusion of randomness.

The Human Temple

> *"The great majority of us are required to live a life of constant, systematic duplicity. Your health is bound to be affected if, day after day, you say the opposite of what you feel, if you grovel before what you dislike and rejoice at what bring you nothing but misfortune. Our nervous system isn't just a fiction, it's part of our physical body, and our soul exists in space and is inside us, like teeth in our mouth. It can't be forever violated with impunity."*
>
> Boris Pasternak (1890 - 1960), Doctor Zhivago

The Size of Humans: Why?

There is relevance to the dimensions of planets in relation to humans, just as there is relevance to the dimensions of cells in relation to atoms. The relationships are contingent upon function. One entity will operate proficiently, given the certain size of its subordinate entities. Entities that do not fit within these operational parameters are not functional and dissolve in the wake of evolutionary conformity. The sustainability of one element in relation to its subordinate element is the key to understanding structural and functional relationships within the universe. Constituencies that form an element share a functional and structural hierarchal relationship.

Justifying the physical sizes of objects requires an examination of the extremes, from the smallest of elements to the largest of masses. Understanding all the small pieces that compose the larger ones reveals the scope of sizes for all elements within existence. For instance, when creating a toy building block structure, the smallest pieces should not be used to build an extremely large model. The structure will become unstable, and several smaller pieces will have to be replaced with larger blocks. Using larger blocks at the base creates a more stable structure that is suitable to the laws that govern its cohesion. Creating a structure with optimal integrity is crucial to the structure's sustainability. Matter is structured through a series of smaller elements that build up substance to ensure its integrity. These elements form a hierarchy of substance, where the lower level elements combine to form substances found higher in the hierarchy. This hierarchy illustrates the reason for a substance's size and function within the universe. If matter were to fall out of order in the hierarchy and become any other size, its integrity and function would diminish.

The evolution of substances ensures that elements are the correct size in order to function within the universe; the sizes of things are a direct relation to an element's function. Only a precisely shaped puzzle piece will fit into the appropriate spot, and so, too, objects in the universe comply with an appropriate form in order to fit in. Pieces that do not comply with this order wilt in the face of evolution. Humans have an elaborate function that requires a unique shape in order to fit within the hierarchy. The function of humanity requires humans to interact with several elements, making the size of humans an elaborate measurement. Evolution has designed humans within a specific size in order to operate optimally in the universe. The study of the human function in relation to existence reveals rationale behind the size of humans.

Rationalizing the human size entails the study of the entire universe in relation to humanity. This process includes the approximate measurement of the extremes within existence. Human progress involves the discovery of the universe; therefore, humans have been granted the tools to explore and experience these extremes. The tools granted to undertake this adventure are configured at an optimal size in order for humans to experience all of the universe's extremes. From the smallest elements to the longest distances, the human size is ideally calibrated in order to facilitate its function. The human stature is relevant to the physical size of the universe, starting from the extravagant and ending with the finest constituency. Every aspect of the universe dictates the size of a human in order to accommodate the human experience. For instance, humans are the exact size required to master the terrains of the Earth, Moon, and other planets in our solar system. Any other size would diminish man's optimum level of discovering proficiency. Humans are housed on a planet at such a size as to maximize human progress. No other size would provide us the experience that the universe has to offer.

The Earth's size is ripe for discovery by a creature of human size. If the Earth were larger and contained more dramatic terrain, humans would have been modified to suit those particular conditions. □┼╫ A proportional ratio exists between the size of humans and the size of the Earth. Evolution has created an ideal creature to explore the Earth and discover the elements contained within it. The hundreds of thousands of years of evolutionary refinement have created the ideally suited size for the function of a human. Humans are the size of an ideal instrument suited to experience the general extremes of existence.

Nature is the process of conforming elements within existence to operate at optimal levels. When environments change, nature quickly adapts its inhabitants to optimize them in order to master their new conditions. Humans have been conditioned by nature to carry out functions at an optimal level. As the demand for larger humans increases, nature will accommodate the demand. The demand to overcome circumstances on Earth has created humans of an optimal size. Figure 13 illustrates the optimal size of humans in relation to all other elements within existence. Humans are optimally sized in relation to the extremes of the universe.

Figure 13 — Building Blocks Functionality Ratio

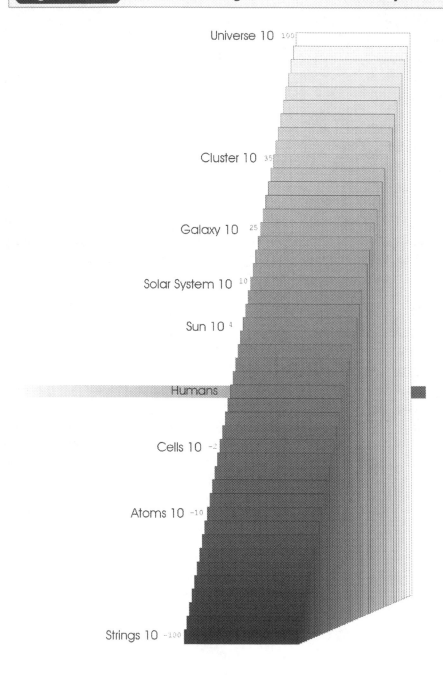

The Design of the Human Body

There are several physical features that distinguish humans from other terrestrial creatures. The human hand has elongated digits with one thumb, a suitable instrument to perform the will of the mind. In order to accommodate an illustrious device such as the mind, the hand has been arranged with five digits, as neither three nor six digits would suffice. A fifth finger would be more suitable for swimming, while three fingers would accommodate a more mobile creature. An ideal medium contrived by evolution has fixed human hands with four fingers. For instance, a dog's paw has small digits suitable for running. The paw's evolution has transformed the ligament into a device more suitable for the needs of a dog. The human hand is an ideal universal tool designed to accommodate the mind's abilities.

The human mind has superior traits over those of its counterpart, the ape. The ability to process memory and resolve algorithms efficiently are just a few examples of humans' superior intellectual abilities. Evolution has developed bodies suitable to house each species proficiently. Every animal has a suitably structured body that complements the capabilities of the mind housed within it. If the mind attains new abilities, the body will, in time, take advantage of the new feature. The body supplies the instruments in relation to the mind's abilities. As the mind evolves, the body will follow suit. Ingrained in the mind and all other cells within the body is an automated program that manipulates the host in accordance to the requirements of sustainability. This program creates diversity within nature and constitutes the harmony of life on Earth. In order to preserve the host, the body contorts to utilize the host's most predominant feature. This process creates advantages over other creatures, ensuring the survival of the host and its offspring. The mind, being a human's most predominant feature, becomes something the body must accommodate in order to sustain the species. ⊔⊦⊦⊦ The body is a reflection of the mind's persona, as its features facilitate the optimal capabilities of the mind. Evolution provides physical amenities to complement the human mind.

91

The mind has several facets, including the ability to absorb information and manipulate data efficiently to produce rational output. In order for the mind to operate proficiently, it requires inputs from the experiential world. The body is an ideal vessel designed to absorb experiences and relay data back to the mind for processing. The body has senses to identify the material world and to relay that sensorial information efficiently to the mind so that it may be absorbed. As the mind becomes more efficient, the body transforms in order to accommodate it, thereby attaining the highest levels of proficiency from the enhanced abilities. The modern era has shown that those who are proficient in their thinking will prosper. Those with efficient minds dominate the species, allowing those with superior thoughts to flourish. This cascading process forces the hand of evolution to produce offspring with the natural ability of enhanced thought. A wave of change sweeps through the species, creating generations of proficient thinkers. In the same light, the same process creates a proficient body to accommodate the mind. The transformation of species will occur with the introduction of the mind's new abilities.

The Equilibrium of Discovery

There are tools designed for each trade. A mechanic's toolbox contains specific tools for various duties. In order to be practical, some tools are utilized for a broader range of applications. For instance, an automobile mechanic will have a screwdriver capable of turning several sized screws. Similarly, creatures from the natural world are granted tools suited to assist them in a variety of applications. These tools complement and assist the creatures in their survival and function. These tools exemplify the creature's purpose by defining a scope for its function. The scope defines which tasks the creature would be most proficient in accomplishing and which tasks are unattainable. The applications for a creature's abilities define its role in the world and its function in relation to its environment.

Humans have several functional attributes that can be applied to a broad range of applications. Each attribute has an equilibrium, a point where the optimal utilization of the tool is apparent. For instance, the human eye is configured to experience a wide spectrum of light. Eyes have never been able to magnify to such a degree as to view particles, nor have they been able to telescope to see across vast distances. Human attributes are ideally tuned to experience the most significant spectrum within the universe. Any other configuration of the human body would lessen the magnitude of experience. If the eye were tuned to a higher level of magnification, humanity would not be able to experience things from greater distances. Although the eye can experience things that are small or large, the optimal spectrum for the eye is that of the broadest spectrum.

The spectrum at which the human eye perceives existence is of the broadest, with the ability to efficiently experience other spectrums with the assistance of human ingenuity. Although unable to experience subatomic particles firsthand, technology supplements this handicap by introducing devices that supersede natural limitations. Access to a broad spectrum allows for easy transition to other spectrums through the use of technology. For instance, the concept of electromagnetic waves was brought on by the experience of the magnetic field. Humanity's introduction to the magnetic field was a result of an experience with magnets that opened an opportunity for the mind to conceptualize a device in which to identify the fields. From that invention, humans were able to experience the magnetic field by means of a device, allowing for further scientific study. In order to maximize human experiences by way of the corporeal world, human eyes need to be attuned to a broad spectrum, allowing for the opportunity to study those things just beyond the capabilities of the natural body. If the human eye perceived the world from an insect's perspective, observing other possible spectrums in the universe would be more challenging and therefore less optimal. We would not have the ability to view the smallest constituency or see the farthest planets in the universe. Therefore, the human eye is tuned at its optimum caliber for a creature with the abilities of a human. Limitations beyond the abilities of the natural body provide an opportunity for humanity to overcome. The eyes' limited ability to see over vast distances coaxed the mind to produce devices to overcome this drawback. Limitations of the body give rise to inventions that extend the body's capabilities.

Developments brought on by these restraints ultimately led to the progress of the human race.

Human abilities are designed in accordance to a pre-fixed rate, which accommodates the progression of the human species. ☐—╫╫ The gradual rate of discovery is regulated by the capacity of humanity's ability to physically experience and discover existence. Our inabilities limit us from veering away from the gradual sequential progress required for uniformed progression. The gradual sequence of discovery assists in the moderate understanding of the universe. For instance, the human body is unable to sustain itself under great pressures when at the bottom of the ocean. Discoveries about creatures at the deepest points of the sea are therefore gradual, as humanity creates innovative devices in order to venture down to depths at greater pressures. Children learn in a sequence of stages in the educational system. Skipping grades causes confusion and disorder. Human abilities are limited to allow us to progress at a consistent sequential pace in order to optimize the discovery of existence. Discoveries both great and small are revealed in an orderly fashion as humanity advances.

The limits of human attributes give clues about the extremes of the universe. A ratio of comparable extremes exists for all things in relation to the capacity of human abilities. The rate of humankind's progressive discoveries allows us to see the smallest constituency while at the same instance discovering the farthest galaxy. Our senses experience the opposing extremes in the universe at the same rate due to the equilibrium of human discovery. The starting point for human sensorial perception is of equal distance from the discovery of the extremes in existence. Human senses are positioned at the midpoint of the extremes, allowing for the discovery of the very small and large to occur in similar time frames.

The Mentality of the Body

Humans come in a variety of body types. Bodies have different shapes, sizes, contours, features, weights, and so on. Each body is unique, although similar body types exist. Individuals acquire body types at conception and mold their bodies throughout childhood. Newborns have similar body types and are commonly distinguished by simple measures including weight and sex. Bodies transform throughout the stages of life as they take on more unique attributes. The process of growing is the process of the body conforming into the most suitable body type for its host.

The body reveals insights into an individual's mentality. Given that the body is a vessel of the mind, it is constructively suited to fit the mind's persona. The body is specifically built as an extension of the mind's caliber. A fit body represents a sound and aware mind. The opposite can be said of an overweight or unbalanced body type. The more aware the mind is, the more refined the body will be, creating an ideal vessel to maximize the mind's fluidity. In order to accommodate the mind's mental capacity, the body conforms to optimize the mind's potential. The mind relies on the body, and in return the body accommodates the mind with the same efficiency it exudes. □┤║ You can identify those who are intellectually acute solely by the classification of their body types. An aware mind requires a honed body in order to operate efficiently, whereas an unbalanced body would burden an efficient mind's abilities.

Defining body types in relation to mental capacity enables the categorization of humans. One can characterize the roles individuals play in society based on their mind's capacity and, even more so, their body characteristics. Positions that require substantial problem solving skills are appropriate for bodies that are naturally aligned and have slender builds, and for people who are healthy, acute, and coordinated. Positions requiring minimal skills are occupied by individuals with relatively unbalanced bodies. Every feature of the body reveals some critical element housed in the host's mind. The mind projects physical attributes upon the body, which in turn portrays characteristics found in the mind. The mind and body are conjointly suited and complement each other's characteristics.

The mind is constantly dictating the body's shape. Minds change with time, and the effects of this change are reflected upon the body. As the mind is refined, it shifts the body's comfort point, willing the body to conform to the mind's current state. Some individuals resist this natural change and oppose the influence of the mind. This resistance causes a constant struggle between the body and the mind, but inevitably the mind wins. For instance, a long distance runner past his prime must will himself to practice, whereas a natural runner will find practicing enjoyable. The body of a natural runner will maintain a slender build without effort, whereas other runners have to work diligently to condition their bodies. A bodybuilder must struggle to condition his muscles, resisting the great urge to rest. The natural tendency of the mind tells the body that the extra muscles are not needed and deters the individual with greater resistance. The mind dictates the course of the body as the individual resists the will of the mind.

The Mind Defines the Body

Humans are drawn to individuals with charisma, personality, and appealing appearances. Natural beauty is appealing, and humans often try to attain this quality through artificial means. Humans are judgmental by nature and are quick to judge on appearances, which dictate future interactions. The media associates success with those who possess attractive qualities. Judging a book by its cover is a human condition, but there are some underlying truths behind this tendency. Humans instinctively judge the attractiveness of all substances to determine if they are favorable or not. Our primal instincts reinforce these judgments and tell us that if a thing looks good, it is good, and that it is more likely to be bad when it looks bad. By nature this is true; humans are only abiding by their nature when making these seemingly rash decisions. Individuals with appealing qualities are naturally more substantial.

The body is a reflection of the mind, and vice versa. ☐⊢⊣⊢ The body is the temple of the mind and is a reflection of its state and condition. Psychological and behavioral traits found in individuals are revealed through the contours, shape, and features of the body. The judgment of a person's character can be passed based on physical features found throughout the body. The physical shape of certain body parts reveals the nature and character of an individual.

The key characteristics of an individual's personality are developed during childhood. Children develop behaviors and personalities that carry over to adulthood. The characteristics humans develop during childhood mold their physical features in the form of developing tissue. Any body parts that contort during childhood are susceptible to the mind's manipulation. The mind manipulates body parts that adjust or mature during the life of the body. The mind projects the contours of certain facial and body features to resemble the physiological state of the mind. These facial and body features are representations of the behavior and character found within all humans that exhibit similar physical features. Those who share similar body conditions possess similar behavioral traits. Categorizing an individual's behavioral patterns can be accomplished by grouping individuals with similar body features.

The mind regulates the stature of the body. It conveys the conditions of the individual and transforms the body appropriately to those conditions. As the mind carries on with its routine operations, the body physically adjusts to conform to the mind's condition. The physical body regenerates itself periodically and takes on new forms based on the mind's blueprints. Some of the apparent features of the body that identify the condition of the mind are facial features (including the shape of nose, cheek, and ears) and body features (including weight, tissue alignment, contour of body, and so on). Every human's body and face are unique, just as every mind is unique in its character. The uniqueness of an individual's face is formed by the distinctive condition of his or her mind. For example, suppressed societies living under a similar mind-set will exhibit similar facial and body conditions. Individuals from isolated societies that harbor similar behaviors will develop comparable features, making them regionally identifiable.

Several behavioral characteristics can be identified by examining specific physical features of the body. The body reveals behavioral traits including temper, patience, coherency, intelligence, and so on. In general, human behavior can be mapped according to features found on the body. Individuals who share similar behaviors have similarly identifiable facial features. Identical twins that have different personalities will have unique facial and body features that reflect their unique behaviors. Close siblings who share similar behaviors will have identical facial features. Finding an individual with similar values equal to your own involves finding someone who looks like you.

Identifying which physical features relate to which behavioral traits allows for a personality categorization of individuals and for segregating classes of humans. Primary segregation begins with the identification of coherency levels of individuals. The level of coherency in an individual can be determined and therefore categorized. Segregating these physical features allows for identifying likely roles and statures within society. Optimal role distribution is conditional upon placing individuals in societal positions suited to their behavior. Individuals with patience and poise will be more suitable for dealing with finance and security. Easily tempered and excited individuals might be more beneficial for military and labor-intensive careers. Aligning individuals to roles with similar behavioral traits calibrates society for optimal performance.

Body features give us an insight into the physiological traits found in each person. Those who hide their bodies are unconsciously hiding their character and inadvertently concealing their behavioral traits. The window into the condition of the mind begins with the state of the body. Closing this window reveals those who harbor behavioral abnormalities. Humanity instinctively perceives concealment as suspicious, and those who hide physical features are those who wish to mask abnormal behaviors.

The Pyramid of Roles

Within a beehive colony there are classifications for the different statures of bee, which designate their duties. These classifications depend upon the different builds of bee, making each bee suitable for his function within the colony. The honey-gathering bees are lighter for better transport, while guardian bees are larger with a greater ability to defend the queen. Like bees, humans have classifications beyond those labeled by social designations. Humans are programmed to perform one duty more effortlessly than others. The human body is designed to accommodate one role more proficiently than any other. □─⊞ A hierarchy of classifications exists for humanity, consisting of various roles required for the species to function optimally. The pyramid of specialized roles is comprised of several designations, beginning with scarce roles near the peak of the pyramid and more generalized roles near the base. Some roles found within the pyramid include thinkers, leaders, laborers, technicians, and so on. Highly specialized roles have far fewer participants than generalized roles. Generalized roles are required in larger numbers in order to support those individuals with roles located higher on the pyramid.

A specific number of participants are required for each role in the pyramid in order to keep the organization productive. Each level of roles within the hierarchy supports successive levels and accumulatively supports the entire structure. The purpose behind the pyramid of roles is that it allows for greater achievements toward the goals of humanity. If the roles are adequately filled, the organization becomes more productive and can then reach its objectives quicker. Humanity can progress more rapidly when participants are properly assigned to their optimal roles. The organization operates efficiently when the pieces of the engine are properly aligned. With adequate role fulfillment on the lower levels of the pyramid, individuals striving to satisfy roles higher on the pyramid can achieve greater feats. Efficiency begins at the foundation and flows through the roles at the peak of the pyramid.

Roles are systemically filled as the requirements are realized. If there are not enough participants in a specific role, nature finds a way to replenish this necessity. The demands for a certain amount of participants in each role are met through the course of *progressive adaptation*. When deficiencies arise, nature relies upon this system to replenish shortages. Scarcities bring about the demand for resources, to which progressive adaptation supplies. This is nature's way of filling in the pieces of the puzzle in order to make the operation of nature run efficiently.

Specialization allows for greater efficiency and the enrichment of each role. Individuals who specialize in certain roles produce greater achievements, making humanity more productive. These specialized roles materialize as requirements arise. Specializations allow for populations to be less self-reliant and more dependent on a conglomeration of skills. Self-reliance is minimized as each individual requires fewer skills for all things and more skills for one thing. Populations operate as components of a machine, with one unit focusing its efforts on one objective, knowing that the other priorities are being cared for. The greater the population, the more specialized it becomes as roles are divided into more specific functions. The population meets the demand for specialization as required by the society. Those who overspecialize or underspecialize must adjust to comply with demand.

Roles are not assigned, but rather individuals are born into their roles and are refined during childhood. Genetic influences play a part in the assignment of roles, including circumstantial conditions and responses to requirements. When the requirements of certain roles reach a threshold, those roles will be filled exponentially. The circumstances of the previous generations dictate the roles that will be filled by the next generations. Childhood is the process of refining skills required for role fulfillment, although individuals designated for a specific role may neglect their intended designation and pursue another activity. For instance, a guardian bee can choose to gather honey instead and become mediocre in the task. Characteristics and qualities are attained during childhood in preparation for intended roles. This process allows some adults to have better tendencies to lead, while others have a better tendency to think or to work with mechanical devices. During the course of life, individuals find suitable labor, suitable partners, and suitable environments that nurture their intended roles.

The majority of the human population subscribes to roles associated with the lower portion of the role pyramid (see Figure 14). Only a fraction of the population has the ability to fulfill a role located in the upper echelons of the pyramid. The majority of human progress is led by those who fulfill roles located in the upper echelons. Although the roles associated with the lower portion of the role pyramid contribute little to the progress of humanity, they are required in larger numbers to support the individuals fulfilling higher-level roles. Human progress requires large numbers of humans to be laborers, a few must be leaders, and a rare few will be thinkers. The collective powers of humans engaged in a task are realized when several roles work in unison to attain one feat. Consider the feat of placing a man on the Moon. Several layers of skills were required to accomplish this task. The project required several designers, who were supported by technicians who built the rocket components. Tasks were efficiently designated and achieved as individuals worked to their optimal ability toward realizing one goal.

Society labels individuals based on their wealth, stature, career, and so on. Humanity's natural roles transcend these categorizations, as they are defined through mental criteria. Roles are defined by the mental integrity of an individual. The capabilities of the mind define whether individuals reside in the lower or upper echelons of the role pyramid. The mind is the device regulating the role an individual is capable of fulfilling.

Figure 14 Pyramid of Roles

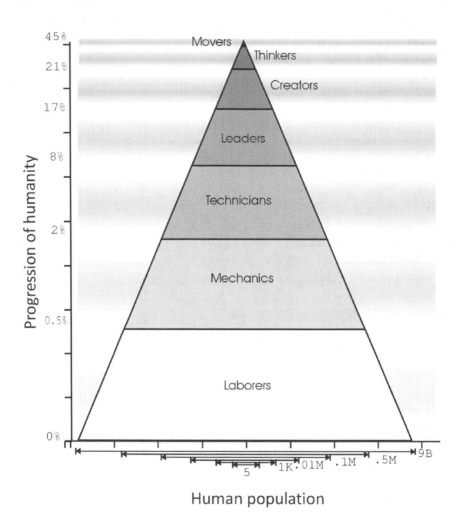

Human population

The Mind Shapes the Body

The body is a puppet controlled by the mind. When humans want to change the condition of their body, they must initially change their state of mind. A healthy mind equates to a healthy body. Those who have defects in the body essentially have abnormalities in the mind that perpetuate those defects. Conditioning the mind conforms the body. Individuals who deceive the mind with a surreal reality can manipulate their bodies into equally surreal states. For example, medical miracles are situations where the mind is deceived into a surreal condition, and this new condition is then reflected onto the body. Convincing the mind to conform to a new reality requires concentration. Concentration is the practice of subduing inherent instinctive impulses that distract our focus. People in civil societies are taught to concentrate and to practice controlling impulses prior to making judgments. Civil people do not react to situations instantly, but rather take a moment to analyze the correct response. These lessons are conveyed throughout childhood as children are taught to suppress their emotions and to concentrate on their actions.

Revealing one's true nature is an unconventional practice in business circles. Businesspeople practice masking their personal motives. Successful businesspeople are perceived as those who are in control and who avoid impulsive and emotional judgments; they maintain an air of calm and poise. Habits and traits acquired throughout childhood are shelved in preparation for the succession to adulthood. The mind enters a ritualistic custom wherein the individual forces a condition upon the mind that goes against the mind's natural tendencies. Imposing conditions upon the mind comes in the form of will, forcing compliance of ideal social norms. Personal traits and the shape of the body conform to social norms, thereby placing the mind under arrest. Individuals are constantly contorting the natural tendencies of the mind to comply with foreign conditions. The will of the individual overpowers the natural tendencies of the mind until the resistance gradually dissipates.

Acting requires trained thought, and maintaining that thought requires concentration. When concentration is lost, actions resort to instincts derived from personal traits. These instinctive behaviors are the windows into revealing an individual's true character. By examining instinctive reactions, we can piece together the type of personality and mind-set an individual possesses. Instinctive reactions are exposed when actions rely less upon analytical thought and more upon impulses. These reactions are more likely to be exposed during mundane activities that require little concentration including driving, balancing, walking, and the like. They are also identified in actions where emotions override reasoning, including impatience, posture, and attitude. Behavioral traits are a reflection of a human's mental state. Every movement and every reaction exemplifies some trait possessed by the mind.

A child is a blank canvas waiting to absorb influences from the experiential world. From birth, children have relatively the same physical and mental stature. As they age, they encounter traits that are absorbed by the mind. These traits mature and transform into a personality. The body is a constantly changing mechanism that completely renews itself throughout the year. The only unchanging substances within the body are the characteristics stored within the mind. These nonphysical substances exemplify the individual through thoughts, experiences, personality, and skills. The mind is the central core that houses the architectural design of the body, which distinguishes one person from another. □┤┼┤ Every person is a walking representation of his or her mind-set. The puppeteer adopts a suitable puppet to exemplify its abilities.

Religious Substance

> *"The principle of liberty and equality, if coupled with mere selfishness, will make men only devils, each trying to be independent that he may fight only for his own interest. And here is the need of religion and its power, to bring in the principle of benevolence and love to men."*
>
> John Randolph (1773 - 1833)

Prayer, the Channel to God

Prayer is the process of focusing on thought and conforming the mind. It consists of sensory depravation, concentration, and repetitive thought. We close our eyes, isolate ourselves, lose touch with our physical surroundings, and concentrate on phrases. Concentrating on thought separates an individual from the sensorial world, leaving him or her with unadulterated thoughts. When secluded from reality, the mind manufactures a new reality like those found in our dreams. The mind's dynamics allow for reality to be re-created by inducing simulated sensorial experiences. The vivid reality produced in the mind is indistinguishable from actual reality. Prayer is a conduit to a new reality, one that an individual can consciously provoke.

Prayer is a release from reality and provides a sense of therapeutic serenity. A detachment from reality alleviates an individual's psychological tensions and creates a remedy for reducing the strain brought about by reality. This remedy produces a perceived reality and transforms physical reality into the realm of the perceived reality. ▢─╫ In order to transform perceived reality into physical reality, the subject has to convince the mind that the perceptions are real. This process involves believing wholeheartedly in a perception and its concepts. The power in the remedy lies in the ability of the subject to convince the mind that something is true, although it cannot be physically experienced. This technique involves inducing the mind through a process of conformity. Conforming the mind involves changing the mind's perceived reality to one that suits the host. The process of conformity involves overwhelming the mind with concepts of the new reality by introducing physical and physiological experiences that reinforce it. There are several methods for conforming the mind and adopting a new reality. By manipulating a subject's experiences and circumstances, the mind becomes conditioned to an alternate reality. The subject is then influenced by physical and physiological evidence, which reinforces the credibility of the perception. For instance, by surrounding a subject in a place that promotes this new reality, the mind is more susceptible to believe in it. Once the new reality becomes credible, the mind is able to adopt the new perspective.

Our reality is easy to believe because we experience it throughout our lives. If we were to experience a dream-like state for an extended period of time, like in a coma, our dreams would become our reality. The reality with the greatest influence takes precedence, and the more we experience it, the more real it seems. The more real an experience is, the easier it is for the mind to believe it. Prayer and religion are most potent when practiced consistently. Prayer imposes its greatest influence when consistently persuading the subject. Repetition is the key to prayer; the more times it is experienced, the more believable it becomes. By repeating prayers, the concepts become ingrained into the consciousness, making them more easily believable, thereby easily manifesting into reality. The more real you create a perspective in reality, the more believable it is. The practice of prayer increases the exposure to the new reality, making it conceivable.

Developing your own reality is beneficial. By conforming the mind, you can manipulate reality into producing perfect health, immense strength, speed, and so on. The body can transform into a desirable condition as dictated by the mind. Hypnosis is an extreme form of mind control and is often applied to patients who want to cure a physical ailment. This remedy works if the subject believes in the solution. Hypnotizing someone to jump like a cheetah every time they jump will produce minimal immediate results. After several years under this influence, the individual will be able to jump farther and will have developed stronger legs, even though the individual has had no physical training. The mind has gradually conformed the body, given the new perspective implanted into the mind. The manipulation of perceived reality can transform into actual reality with practice and time.

The Path to God

Religions state that the evidence of God is existence itself. God is attributed to creation and is identified with those things that cannot be explained. Man uses God to make life more convenient, and the closer God is to His subjects, the more convenient life is. Meditation and prayer are the channels of communication with God. They entail detaching oneself from sensorial experiences and focusing on thought. God exists in thought and more so in the mind. The closer we are in touch with thought, the closer we are to grasping the notion of God. Sensory deprivation is required to get in tune with our thoughts. Focusing on thought enhances our perceptual understanding of the corporeal world and brings us closer to an understanding of the universe. ☐—╫ To get closer to an all-knowing God, we study thought, thereby improving our knowledge, which builds a path that delivers us to God. Once the goal of understanding the universe is attained, we will be equal to its creator.

The practice of knowledge is the process of reaching God. The more we understand the methodology of the creator, the closer we come to knowing Him. Once we understand the makings of the universe, God's plan for us will be revealed. We only have bits and pieces of the puzzle, evidence of some logic about how things work. By discovering new knowledge about existence, the puzzle begins to form a picture. As we complete this puzzle, the momentum increases and pieces begin to align more fluently as the picture of the universe becomes legible. Knowledge will bring us closer to the solution of the puzzle. Knowledge is the path that will lead us to God.

Knowledge is efficiently acquired when an individual is focused on thought and isolated from the corporeal world. Isolation is the vehicle leading to the mastery of thought. Leave a man on a deserted island and he will become the master of his universe. When you have no one to answer to, you are the ruler of your world. The more secluded you become, the more in tune you will be with your thoughts and the closer you will be to becoming a supreme being. The world beyond your mind is there to occupy your attention. If you fall prey to its seduction, you will lose yourself in the human experience. The observation, analysis, and regurgitation of reality must be balanced to coincide with humanity's objective of enlightenment. A meaningful life is unattainable if you are just observing the picture show of existence.

> *"If thou desire the love of God and man, be humble, for the proud heart, as it loves none but itself, is beloved of none but itself. Humility enforces where neither virtue, nor strength, nor reason can prevail."*
>
> Francis Quarles (1592 - 1644)

How Real Is God?

There is no certainty in the material universe, as matter is susceptible to change. The physical world is constantly evolving, creating slices of existence for our experience. Things that are known to be certain are thoughts derived from the mind. You are certain when you think your own thoughts. The mind is the center of your universe, and things that influence your mind contain a degree of certainty. Influences from the sensorial world that manipulate your thoughts contain an element of certainty. There is a hierarchy of certainty granted to those things that substantially influence the mind and to those things that do not. ☐┼╫ Those things that directly influence the mind have a higher degree of certainty. Influences that significantly manipulate your thoughts are more certain to exist. You are justified in saying that whatever influences your mind contains a degree of certainty.

You can tangibly qualify that God is real by the influence He has on humanity. The greatest influence on Earth is God, exemplified by the actions of humanity. He is an object of great influence, wielding devoted disciples and modifying human behavior. The popularity of God is renowned, as everywhere you travel people know who He is. Symbols of Him are found in temples and buildings throughout the world. He is referenced in anthems and books. If an alien from another planet were to visit Earth, he would likely consider God as our leader. Societies regularly strive to follow the directions set out by God.

Although emotions cannot be physically held in the hand or touched, they exist. Emotions are an experience conjured by the mind and can only be felt by the person who feels them. Man has the ability to manifest his thoughts into reality. The mind can manipulate the experiential world, which becomes real if only through the individual experiencing the perception. In the same sense, God is of the same nature. We cannot touch, hold, or see Him, but He exists in the mind. God exists simply by the influence He has on humanity. The greatest influence on man is God, and the majority of Earth's population agrees that He exists. People's lives are affected by God, and He influences their existence. The concept of God can induce mental and physical changes in a subject. When we think about God, it causes a behavioral change in us. The thought of God manifests itself into physical reality through the actions of man. The nonphysical world has been a part of existence since the conception of man and gains momentum the more humanity relies on it.

Behind the Looking Glass

God is described using immeasurable adjectives, an entity beyond reality, everlasting and perfect. These values do not correspond with objects in the material universe, as the universe is imperfect and constantly changing. An entity existing within the universe would have to abide by the universe's principles. God exists on a higher plane beyond that of the universe, one that cannot be influenced by matter, but rather projects influences upon physical things. There are several infallible things that exist within this category, namely the principles governing existence. These principles consist of universal truths that dictate the course of matter. These mathematical equations do not tangibly exist, but influence the behavior of the material universe. They are fixed and never changing, consistent and everlasting, and exist without physical form.

God is an observer through a looking glass who does not interact with His subjects. □┤╫ The infallible God exists beyond the experiences of man. If God were to reveal Himself, it would diminish His image and grandeur. Humans are critical by nature and have a tendency to diminish the value of tangible things. Things that one can touch and feel are subject to flaws by subjective minds. Absolute truths are not subject to opinions, but rather are accurate or inaccurate. Without a specific object to define, God exists in perfection if only in our minds, an almighty being that has no physical substance but is so relevant to human lives that He ritually dictates human actions.

Similar to universal truths, God serves humanity as a necessity, defining existence. Where the explanations for the interaction of physical bodies have failed, God intervenes with purpose to define the indefinable. For instance, the explanation of Earth's solar system was defined by God's will until principles defining the movements of celestial bodies arose. God continually remains a plausible explanation of existence until a better explanation is provided. God is associated with good things and serves several functions for humanity. If God stays above the clouds and is never humanized, His prevalence will be sustained. As soon as God enters the physical world, He will no longer hold the title of God.

God Interpreted

The history of humanity has produced the presence of a variety of gods, each accompanied by their own philosophies. The gods represent different beliefs and provide a service within the society for those who worship them. The methodologies of the gods came from the translations of the inhabitants who follow them. These methodologies are translated through humans, as humans attempt to interpret the concepts of the gods. The gods' abilities are limited by the imagination of human conceptualizations. The gods' abilities are those of the ideas conjured by humans that define their prowess. Abilities associated with gods vary based on the condition of the interpreter and the society's circumstances for which the interpreter resides. The gods' presence and abilities are more powerful in the wake of despair and less potent in times of prosperity. Their abilities are conditional, adapting and changing to the times, giving rise to new venues of salvation as they are required. Religion becomes a conforming service that accommodates its followers, given the society's needs.

Throughout history, humanity has interpreted laws, punishments, and methodologies on behalf of gods. A god is a being with no physical presence and who is defined with broad interpretations. In order for the gods to be relevant, they have to be relevant to the society following them, thereby giving the gods credibility and purpose. Science cannot refute the claims that a god exists, as the notion of a god is associated with infinity, limitlessness, and all-encompassing values that cannot be measured quantifiably. Science can only critique scriptures written by man defining god. Scientists critique the laws that regulate the religion as they conflict with the jurisdiction of science. The laws of god accommodate the times, reinforcing the relationship with its followers. Conditions of religious laws are based on the necessities of the followers, which essentially dictate the reforms of governing laws. If the service becomes out of touch with the followers, the god will become obsolete and eventually will be neglected. In order for one entity to exist with another, the relationship must stay relevant and functional.

God's presence with humanity is based on a popular concept that provides a valuable service to the followers. The value of a god dictates its influence and the role it plays with the population. ☐┤╫ Individuals perceive the role and function of gods uniquely, as gods are accorded different values and perform different services for each individual. Although methodologies are clearly written about the concept of god, each individual perceives God differently. For instance, there is a difference between the way I perceive God and the way you perceive God. Both perceptions are correct, but serve us uniquely. The value of the service is in accordance with the presence God portrays to each individual. God is a generic service that individuals pull various values from. Individuals call upon God for various services during times of need, poor health, misfortune, discomfort, lack of security, and disorder. God represents something unique to each individual, as each individual uses God uniquely in relation to his or her needs. The rules of God conform to each interpretation and represent a service subjected to the individual. Although the image of God may be similar between individuals, His concepts are not.

Although God is an absolute being, humanity does not have an absolute definition for God. Every individual perceives God in a different light. Beyond what religions teach individuals about God, our personal experiences with God form a unique conception. Individuals use God in various ways, redefining His function for each individual. God is a conforming instrument serving individuals uniquely, continually redefining his function. For instance, visiting an amusement park brings about unique feelings of excitement. After visiting the same amusement park several times, your opinion of the park changes as the excitement you once felt diminishes. Every experience with God changes your conception of Him. God is an inanimate being and adopts a unique conception wielded by an individual's perception, which is ultimately based on his experiences.

God's Form and the Image of Man

The form of God has been debated throughout history. Some religions maintain that God made man in His own image. This interpretation articulates that humans must be in the form of a perfect being, but this is not the case. Creatures on Earth serve a function, and their bodies have evolved to perform these functions proficiently. The human body is a changing tool that conforms, given earthly circumstances. For instance, a snake has the ability to capture rodents efficiently and in abundance. Without the presence of snakes, parts of the world would be overrun with rodents, thereby calling upon evolution to supplement the absence of a snake. The structure of a snake is designed to suit a purpose, and the same can be said about other creatures on Earth, including humans. Humans have a unique function unlike other creatures or beings, including God. The functions of humanity and God are unalike; therefore, they do not have the same design.

Evolution has molded the human body to be proficient for a specific purpose that is unlike the purpose of God. Until humans adopt a godly function, their bodies will continue to take on a form optimal for a subordinate function.

In order to define God's physical structure, you have to identify the function of God. The function defines the form. The form will be of the most optimal design in order to accommodate the function. Religion defines God's function as the creator of all life and existence. God is all-knowing and all-powerful, with the ability to control all aspects of life. □┤┼┤ The form of God is of a functional device that suits His purpose. The human portrayal of God is pursued to accommodate the human ego. God then takes on a human form, which humans can then identify with. The physical perception of God heightens His relationship with humans and serves as bridge to appease the human ego.

There are several interpretations for the image of God, but the majority of religious interpretations portray God with the features of man. Therein, the portrayal of God consists of elements found on Earth, namely those of the human body. Although never physically seen, God adopts the image scripted by the religion that is praising Him. There are no fixed perceptions of God, although He is scripted as being unchangeable. God and His image are forever changing in the perception of man. God is limited only by the imagination of man and by the regulations of the religion governing Him. God takes shape out of convenience for His followers. As religions change their regulations, so too does the image of God in order to correspond with the needs of the followers. For instance, it is in the best interest to modify structures within a city to accommodate its citizens. The metamorphosis of the city is guided by consensus. Religions abide by a consensus of their followers in order to accommodate them.

The Yearning for a Guardian

Children learn about the world from guardians. Knowledge possessed by guardians is taught to successive generations. Children born in the twenty-first century are more educated than those of the nineteenth century simply because their guardians are more knowledgeable. The progress of humanity relies on the ability of guardians to pass on knowledge acquired from previous generations. Children instinctively seek out guardians for enlightenment, and particularly those guardians with substantial knowledge. Humanity would be unsuccessful if each generation had to reinvent the experiential world in order to teach successive generations. In this scenario, the world would be frozen in a knowledge time loop, with every life lesson taught being forgotten and retaught each day. The human population would become stagnant, with little emphasis on development. A return to mundane tasks for survival would ensue.

Humanity was put on Earth with no knowledge or guardians. No one taught early humans the ways of the world or the universe. Like lost children, humans searched for answers they could not explain and yearned for a father figure to guide them. With no guide, humanity invented knowledge and began the process of self-learning. As self-awareness became prevalent, the psychological void for a mentor escalated. A ceremonious guardian was conceptualized that fulfilled the growing void. □⊢⊩ As the mind matured, the requirement for a god materialized, providing understanding to those things beyond humanity's conceptual scope. A relationship with a supreme being materialized to appease the distress of the mind.

The yearning for a guardian exists in humans and is more evident in some individuals than in others. A god fulfills multiple psychological voids within the human mind, thereby appeasing the human condition. The prevalent void within man makes it a necessity for humans to endlessly pursue a relationship with a higher power. As long as the void exists within the human mind, a god will be relevant to humankind. For example, a child without parents will instinctively seek out an authority figure. As long as humans are not the masters of their own realm, they will yearn for a superior being to mentor them.

Humans will continue to ponder questions that only a guardian would be able to provide.

The Perception of Morality

There are standards of morality that vary between societies. Each society has its unique definition of morality that is derived from the consensus of its inhabitants. Laws governing morality dictate the lifestyle of a society and reflect upon traits found within local religions. Governments base their policies on beliefs that are upheld by the population, thereby reinforcing the sanctity of religious policies. Morality is reinforced by law and nurtured by beliefs. As religions and laws vary between countries, so too do the standards of morality.

Considered flawless, God has no morality or the ability to judge good from bad. God is a perfect being who has created a perfect world with perfect subjects. A perfect subject cannot commit immoral acts in the eyes of God; therefore, if humans kill or love, the moral implications of these acts are nonexistent and uncontested. Human actions are conducted in accordance with their design and do not impeach their nature. Every action by man is done by the natural tendencies instilled in him by his creator. All actions are considered justly and do not weigh favorably in one direction in the eyes of God. Morality is a human invention and is subject to human opinions. Judgments made on defining the benchmarks of morality are jaded by personal opinions. Morality is applicable to those who abide by its benchmarks. For instance, if I want to be treated in a certain moral manner, I must abide by those same moral standards and treat all others by these benchmarks. Those with lower moral standards and who treat people harshly should expect to be treated harshly under inferior moral standards. Morality becomes a device within a society for legislating the behavior of its citizens.

It is the nature of the beast to do all things its mind wills it to do. Wild animals in the jungle will kill for survival or for other motivations. This behavior is not considered immoral, as it is in the nature of the creature to act this way. Creatures are programmed to perform in a certain manner, in accordance with their design, in order to fit into the puzzle of existence. Humanity is a piece of the puzzle designed to function as humans do in order to fit optimally within existence. Human actions are in tune with their nature, similar to those of wild animals. God looks upon human actions as natural and within the confines of human nature. ☐┤┼┤ There are no right or wrong actions in the eyes of God, as all actions are in accordance with the species' design.

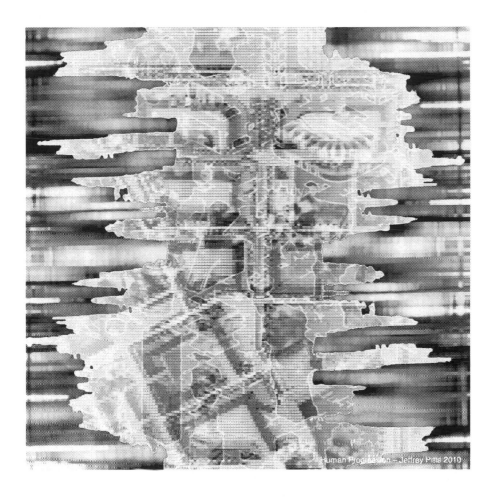

Human Progression – Jeffrey Pitts 2010

Part 2 Human Progression

Change is an irreversible process that forces progress forward. Humanity has been progressing ever since it came into being and will continue to progress. There is an agenda reinforcing human progress and with those elements involved in supporting this intention. The universe is evolving and humanity is evolving with the universe. Humanity has become an extension of the transforming process within the universe ever since it came into being. Evolution has entered a new phase, as human beings have become empowered with knowledge and with the ability to mitigate their own evolution. Humanity has inevitably changed with time. The state of early man has undergone a tremendous, irreversible transformation.

2.1 Subject Keys

Choose your path. Read key statements for every topic and mark those topics of most interest. The subject keys that appeal to you reveal insights into your human nature. Read your selections one after another, then move forward to part 4 to discover insights into your nature and how your selections reflect upon you.

	KEY STATEMENT	pg
■ ○	Humanity has been left on its own to contemplate on how things operate in the universe.	123
	Left to our demise	
■ ○	The rate at which the perceived limits of the universe expand is synchronized with humanity's capacity to comprehend the phenomena.	124
	The perceived boundaries of the universe	
■ ○	Human life is a methodical exercise designed to train the human race in preparation for obstacles.	126
	Progression of obstacles	
■ ○	The lines that separate man from the universe dissolve, as obstacles plundering the universe become humanity's duty to resolve.	128
	Responsibility for obstacles	
■ ○	Each catastrophic event defused by human ingenuity represents another tier of human progression.	129
	Obstacles assist humanity progress	
■ ○	Humans are the universe's greatest attempt towards creating a device to restore its energy.	131
	Universal Regeneration	
■ ○	The degree of change on earth dictates the rate of development for its inhabitants.	133
	The progression of nature on earth	
■ ○	Man has eclipsed evolution and has become the master of his evolving destiny.	136
	The eclipse of evolution	

The Path Laid Out

> *"How far you go in life depends on your being tender with the young, compassionate with the aged, sympathetic with the striving, and tolerant of the weak and the strong -- because someday you will have been all of these."*
>
> George Washington Carver (1864 - 1943)

Left to Our Demise

Humanity has been abandoned, like a survivor on a tropical island, secluded from other civilizations. The desolate Earth is a lavish habitat in the middle of obscurity. □—╫ Humanity has been left on its own to contemplate on how things operate in the universe. Similar to an abandoned child, humanity has been isolated to discover existence without a mentor to educate or a guide to direct. The absence of a teacher has led to the invention of a luminary authoritative figure in order to fill a psychological void. The human mind is built with the capacity to cope with the absence of a guide. Humanity's contrived path of progression is a journey of self-discovery, which entails the discovery of its own destiny.

Humans possess a unique ability: to question their own existence. The human mind constantly ponders as existence displays spectacular scenarios that conjure questions about life. Understanding the scheme of existence requires ample knowledge, which was required by the human species to invent. The ways of the world had to be acquired through experiences. Human beings began to apply the proven method of trial and error in order to define existence and build a database of knowledge. Several scenarios were assumed and played out until the correct one was revealed, which was then recorded for future use. This process required time, which is a characteristic of learning. The advancement of humanity will take time, similar to the increments of time required for a child to advance. Humanity will continue to ponder over its existence and, like children, constantly ask questions about the unknown.

Without some relation to surrounding bodies, the Earth becomes a floating cork in an endless pool of space with no reference to its bearing. The human predicament situates humans on a floating cork in the middle of a sea, unable to perceive the boundaries of existence. Humanity's experience is limited to the expansive space surrounding the Earth, leaving humanity to guess Earth's trajectory and direction. Earth's direction is surmised by the relationships Earth has with other floating objects around it. The Earth exists in relation to other objects and has no point of reference. Earth's mere existence is subject to the relationships it has with other objects. Similar to Earth, humans exist without bearing, unless in relation to another being. Until humanity reaches the proverbial shore of existence, or reaches a certain intellectual maturity, it will continue to exist relatively. Humans are traveling in an unknown direction without a clear destination. This conundrum weighs heavily on the mind, instigating the use of knowledge to unravel the mystery. Knowledge dissolves the mysteries of reality and makes human life substantial. Humanity will continue to ponder over the amazing events within existence until the science behind the picture show of life is unravelled.

The Perceived Boundaries of the Universe

Human perceptions influence reality. Mere speculation on the stock market increases or decreases the value of shares. At one point in time, the limits of the perceived universe were just beyond the reaches of humanity, on the edges of the ocean. This convenient theory was suitable for its time, placing humanity in a significant role in relation to existence. Limiting the grandeur of the universe confines the human species from experiencing those things beyond their comprehension.

Limiting the universe to fixed boundaries eliminates daunting questions about existence and creates a sense of cohesiveness with the universe that makes existence practical. The mind can more easily grasp the logic governing the universe with fixed boundaries rather than with infinites. As humanity progresses and learns more about the universe, the perceived limits of the universe gradually increase. The boundaries continue to extend as new conceptual evidence is revealed. □─┼┼ The rate at which the perceived limits of the universe expand is synchronized with humanity's capacity to comprehend the phenomena.

The edges of the universe reach new boundaries as humanity's understanding of the universe advances. These limits are extended in relation to humanity's amplitude to accept such policies that diminish humanity's significance in the universe. The continual stretching of the universe reveals new possibilities about existence, which sustains human bewilderment. The boundaries of the universe have consistently remained within the bounds of human comprehension. As knowledge accumulates and more mysteries of the universe are resolved, new intriguing discoveries arise automatically, perpetuating human fascination with existence.

From our current perspective, the vastness of the universe is overwhelming, but comprehensible. The universe is expanding at an alarming rate, which physiologically detaches humans from the universe, thereby marginalizing humanity as insignificant observers. Humanity's endeavor to progress has led to technologies that uncover the secrets of the universe, revealing how minuscule the Earth and humans are in relation to the vastness of space. The conceptual widening of existence has led to scientific conclusions that detach humanity from the universe, thereby marginalizing the role of humans in the grand scheme of existence. This detachment widens incrementally with every new scientific discovery, thereby isolating the human species more and more. With every discovery expanding space, humanity is automatically willed to replace the new bewildering findings with logical explanations that strengthen the bond between humans and the universe. For every quantum leap made in astronomy, there are several theories introduced that marginalize space, thereby belittling the universe and making it conceptually manageable.

Theories entailing the coding of existence are made to fit into the palm of your hand, making space less intimidating. These concepts empower humans, making them more significant in the grand scheme of existence. The balance of fitting humanity in a meaningful position within existence is a constant endeavour but a necessary one.

The concept of the universe is overwhelming by design and evolves as humanity progresses. The limits of existence will constantly be out of reach to coax humanity to discover and perceive broader conceptions. Once humanity reaches a boundary, the frontier systematically expands, thereby redefining itself by revealing other new possibilities. Initially, humans saw the oceans as the ends of the Earth. Once this assumption was dismantled, the space existing beyond those limits created more opportunities to accommodate the gradual progress of humanity. Human progress relies upon the attainment of new knowledge. Limiting existence with boundaries therefore limits humanity's potential and dwarfs potential progress. Unlimited boundaries exemplify the concept of unlimited possibilities and unlimited knowledge. The progress of human maturity is in line with newfound opportunities of exploration and discovery. The limits of existence will continue to reveal new avenues to accommodate the limitless appetite of the human mind.

Progression of Obstacles

The universe is abundant with obstacles. Their presence intimidates man but does not deter him. The process of human progression involves the conquest of obstacles through the use of tools that exemplify the human species. Obstacles defying humanity are training exercises that exist to develop human abilities into their ultimate potential. Conundrums develop the human species, therein exercising human mental prowess and building a race of proficient thinkers. This preconfigured gauntlet of obstacles leads humanity toward a progressive path of purpose. ☐⊦⊩ Human life is a methodical exercise designed to train the human race in preparation for obstacles. Humanity's entire environment is devoted to the cause of human progression. Resolutions to obstacles serve as accumulated knowledge that teach future generations and assist in resolving future impediments. These resolutions have a profound purpose and play a role in the scripted universe. Solutions for accumulated obstacles build the library of human knowledge required to advance the human race. Every action having a cause serves as an increment of progress for humanity. Obstacles are justified in the grand scheme for the progression of the universe.

Humanity has been given the means and the will to overcome obstacles. We have been strategically supplemented with resources required to progress and equip with abilities to overcome tribulations. Overcoming obstacles creates a *positive direction of progress* for human achievement. Humanity is able to overcome more prominent obstacles with the passing of time through the accumulation of knowledge. The collective conquests over historic impediments have prepared humanity to overcome sequentially more obtrusive obstacles. These progressive achievements over obstacles are prearranged in a precise order to steadily mature human progression. Each successive impediment increases in difficulty, thereby challenging humanity and providing greater tests of knowledge. The introduction of perpetually grander obstacles assists in motivating humanity to strive for greater heights. More challenging obstacles exude greater rewards, thus sustaining human desire. Foreseeing greater achievements in the wake of more difficult obstacles indicates that man is headed toward the proper path of *progressive obstacles.*

Conquering obstacles redefines and exemplifies humanity's purpose in the universe. Achievements over obstacles become a positive measure of human progress as they condition man to accomplish ever greater feats. As the ultimate goal of humanity becomes clearer with each obstacle surmounted, the definition of humanity becomes refined. The purpose of humanity becomes focused as the collective goal of humanity becomes more prevalent. Humanity retains more purpose and reinforces its place within existence. The universe becomes one with humanity instead of a separate entity.

Responsibility for Obstacles

Humanity has persevered over natural disasters throughout history. The future holds even more devastating disasters, which humanity will overcome. These obstacles are trials for humanity, testing human ingenuity and the maturity level of human progress. Obstacles are the testing grounds that perpetually graduate humanity to higher levels of maturity. When human beings attain the knowledge and experience to overcome pivotal obstacles, they surpass a successive stage of progression and retain a higher stasis as a species. Every substantial feat achieved automatically promotes humanity to another level within existence, which redefines the human race. Prominent obstacles that forge human history are the barriers between humanity attaining successive levels of maturity. The more notable the obstacle conquered, the more humanity progresses as a species.

Obstacles induce human ingenuity and the limitless potential of the mind. The boundless capability of the mind allows humanity to ponder countless solutions in order to unravel forthcoming disasters and ultimately the conundrum of the universe. Every solution used to resolve obstacles accounts for retained knowledge required to decipher subsequent riddles. The building up of knowledge through the conquering of obstacles is the process of preparing humanity for its ultimate feat. As we try to resolve the problem of the universe, we will discover the problem to be our own. ⊡⊣⊩ The lines that separate man from the universe dissolve, as obstacles plundering the universe become humanity's duty to resolve. Humanity inherits the relentless problems of the universe as humanity becomes the universe's problem solving faction. Humanity continually graduates through levels of progression by overcoming domestic obstacles, which perpetuate into obstacles found abroad in the universe. The transition to more perplexing obstacles prepares humanity in order to resolve issues facing existence. The responsibility of resolving issues within existence falls upon humanity.

The ability to resolve the primary issue of the universe lies within human capacity. The gauntlet of obstacles overcome in the past have forged a database of skills that can be used to resolve more daunting obstacles in the future. Humanity progressively surmounts obstacles, one greater than the last, until faced with the ultimate obstacle, the problem with the universe. The maturity level of humanity will reach an end when every obstacle has been dissolved and the knowledge of all existence is acquired. It is the responsibility of obstacles to perpetually test human ingenuity in preparation for the ultimate test.

Obstacles Assist Human Progress

The greatest change in the universe occurred at its conception. Since that time, unrelenting waves of change of varying magnitudes have plagued the universe. The conception of change was brought about by the need for a reform, an alteration from the previous state in order to better the previous state. The universe does not weigh change as good or bad; rather, any change from the current state is a necessity. Change moves in a positive direction, and the more change there is from the current state, the better.

Change is infused with the human condition, as change is critical for human progress. Significant changes of magnitude are more influential upon humanity and are therefore more recognized. Catastrophes are well recorded throughout human history. Those events that have caused the most change upon humanity are events that are highly recorded. Events that have affected the entire human population have assumed a greater precedence and meaning. These changes have resulted in a substantial displacement of the human species. Changes uproot stagnant existence, causing agitation and resulting in a resurgence of existence. Changes progressively lead to improvements and refinement of past conditions. Any changes in abundance, whether perceived as good or bad, are collectively positive as they promote the resurgence of existence. The greater the change, the more opportunity there is for a resurgence. Causing change is in the best interest of humanity and ultimately the universe.

Humanity will continually be challenged by obstacles to stand as a testament to their demise and purpose in the universe. Adverse events are intended to challenge the maturity of man, to bring humanity to the forefront of its ability in order to overcome diversity. Overcoming adverse events requires a collaboration of knowledge and a collection of human abilities. The greater the collaboration, the greater the opportunity of overcoming paramount obstacles. As humanity gains momentum in resolving pivotal obstacles, more deterrent obstacles will arise to test the developed skills of man. More challenging feats will naturally manifest, testing new levels of human progress. Each adversity that is overcome will solidify humanity's purpose and role in the universe.

⬚⊣╫ Each catastrophic event defused by human ingenuity represents another tier of human progression. Adversities overcome by humanity through the collaborative efforts of the entire species are events that qualify as notable stepping-stones for human progress. Cataclysms that were successfully negotiated represent pinnacle moments in history that validate humanity's competence. They are the progressive stepping-stones leading humanity down a scripted path of development. They are a cocktail of calculated events that introduce the next evolutionary step toward humanity's ultimate goal. Each obstacle supplements deficiencies in human knowledge required for humanity to progress to successive levels. For instance, if human beings are lacking in engineering skills, events will occur forcing human beings to improve their knowledge in the specific field. Once adequate levels of knowledge have been attained, humanity advances and becomes prepared for successive trials.

Natural Prosperity

> *"In all things of nature there is something of the marvellous."*
>
> Aristotle (384 BC - 322 BC), Parts of Animals

Universal Regeneration

The beginning of the universe was a cataclysmic event. The universe had lost its consolidated energy at the moment of the Big Bang. The universe woke up to a shattering explosion that divided its substance into space. The universe was in desperate need of a device to restore itself to its former glory, but no device was readily available. This necessity sparked the process of change called *universal regeneration,* which has been transforming the universe to this day. The universe contains an underlying code that is able to initiate the process of self-regeneration. Since the beginning of change, universal regeneration has begun formulating existence in an attempt to resist the dispersal of energy. During the first change of existence, the universe initiated the process of collecting dispersed energy.

The process of universal regeneration is a simple program aimed at developing devices that can collect the most amount of energy efficiently. The universe needs energy-gathering machines aimed at collecting scattered energy across vast distances. These energy-gathering devices need to be proficient so that they can overcome the forces dispersing the universe. These forces include the inflationary force that is unravelling the universe at an accelerated pace. The devices that are efficient in collecting lost energy will thrive and will be provided resources to multiply. Universal regeneration focuses on constantly improving on devices that can harness energy. The survival of a device is dependent upon its ability to collect more energy than other existing devices. The device that can collect the most energy will prevail over other devices of less efficiency.

Universal regeneration aims at constantly developing devices to gather the energy of the universe. Regeneration has created devices to gather scattered energy and return the universe to its original stature. Regeneration continually builds more efficient devices to collect and consolidate energy. Universal regeneration is the direct cause for the formation of matter, fields, and other elements aimed at resisting the dispersion of energy. Fields were created to trap energy into matter, thereby slowing its acceleration. Gravity and black holes were introduced to capture vast amounts of energy, but they lacked effectiveness. As time passes, universal regeneration creates more efficient energy gatherers by reinventing devices. The universe wants to consolidate its energy and will continue to create devices that gather energy until all the energy has been restored.

Humans are the most recent incarnation of the universe in attempts to gather energy. Humanity is the next successive device designed by the universe to consolidate its energy. Since the conception of the first living cell, more proficient creatures have evolved with more prolific means of capturing energy. When the Earth was hospitable, life began collecting energy from the Sun. The Sun's radiating energy was available in vast amounts, so plant life formed mechanisms to gather solar energy. Plants became the dominant stores of energy, and an opportunity arose to harvest this dominant source of energy in the form of herbivores. Once these creatures became greater stores of energy, carnivores were created to gather energy from herbivores. The momentum of energy-gathering devices swamped the Earth, which resulted in bigger and more fertile creatures like the dinosaurs. Each evolutionary creature had greater abilities to harness energy, thereby becoming the dominant species. Creatures that were inefficient energy gatherers perished in the wake of competition. Although the Earth has witnessed grand energy-gathering devices, the latest creation of universal regeneration has eclipsed them all. Humans are the most proficient energy gatherers the Earth has ever encountered. Man's tenacious desire to acquire and possess energy reaches beyond Earth's borders. The refinement of the human species introduces more willing amplitudes to collect energy at unrelenting rates. ☐⊣⊬ Humans are the universe's greatest attempt toward creating a device to restore its energy.

The Progression of Nature on Earth

Objects with mass are susceptible to change. Change within the universe is the driving force behind the process of creation and destruction. Nothing in the physical realm avoids the cycles of change. The cycles of change include the process of degradation and regeneration. These two processes have been the underlying cause for Earth's transformation into what it is now, and what it will be in the future.

☐⊣⊬ The degree of change on Earth dictates the rate of development for its inhabitants. The Earth utilizes its environment to inflict changes upon inhabitants on its surface. The greater the degree of environmental influences inflicted upon the inhabitants, the more dramatic the transformation of those inhabitants. The rate of Earth's development correlates with the severity of environmental influences on its surface. Extreme environmental conditions give rise to rapid growth, while moderate conditions result in inhabitants experiencing stagnation. Creatures that need to adapt to extreme environmental conditions would have to adapt more frequently to changing conditions. The rapidity of Earth's growth accelerates the growth of creatures existing on its surface.

Positive Opportunism creates new organisms in accordance with the rate of growth. With rapid growth, evolution optimizes an organism quickly, but the hastiness leaves the organism with little substance. Substance is acquired through periods of stagnation or rest. It is a period required for the organism to mature into its form. A mature creature has advantages over novel creatures as it has mastered the abilities of its form. Proper maturing allows the organism to expand its species, thereby creating a dominant race. The rapidity of change prevents the process of substance acquisition, leaving creatures in a state of constant growth. A proper rate of change is imposed upon creatures to develop substance and maintain timely development to optimize form.

There are geographical environmental transformations ranging from global alterations to regional alterations. These transformations can influence the growth and progress of every Earthly inhabitant. Environmental factors stimulate growth, including the rate of growth for humans. Human progression may accelerate or remain stagnant, depending on environmental conditions. Human collections progress differently simply based on their geographical location. An area experiencing rapid growth will produce a different quality of human. Some groups of humans would progress hastily while others would retain substance. For example, some groups would be more prone to agility while others would be more proficient in communications. A greater transformation is experienced by those groups that heavily depend upon their immediate environment. Humans who strictly survive on what their immediate environment can provide will be dramatically influenced by changes in their environment and therefore experience rapid optimization.

The precise configuration of Earth's growth variables promotes the accelerated transformation of its inhabitants. The makeup of Earth and its surrounding system allow for creatures to generously flourish. Several species have flourished within a recurring cycle of progression. Beginning with single-celled organisms, followed by the dinosaurs, the Earth's alignment has nurtured the growth of several species. This nourishing growth rate ultimately leads to the implosion of the species. Each era of civilization has faced cataclysmic events that have caused substantial change, therein introducing subsequent stages of Earth's progression. During peak periods of a species' existence, monumental changes occur, causing devastating change and the promotion of evolution. These calculated events accelerated the evolution of a species and the transformation of the universe.

Figure 15 plots the progression of two species and their correlations with environmental changes. The dotted line represents the overall environmental stability (Line B) for the planet, and the solid line (Line C) tracks the overall progression of a species. Species flourish in favorable environmental circumstances (Point D), which inevitably lead to monumental downfalls (Point M). The progress rate of the species quickly follows the environmental changes and drastically drops (Point F), unable to sustain its momentous development (Point E) within a given set of environmental circumstances. The peak growth of a species declines in order to comply with the environmental changes. The regeneration of the environment (Point S) introduces a new era in Earth's progression, ushering in a period of development. The rate of growth follows a specific pace dictated by environmental circumstances.

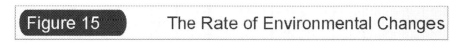

Figure 15   The Rate of Environmental Changes

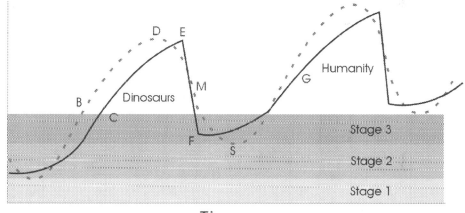

Time

B - Environmental stability
C - Progression of species
D - Peak of environmental stability
E - Peak of species stability and development
F - Collapse of species
G - Regeneration of species

The Eclipse of Evolution

There is a limit to the spectrum and rate in which images can be perceived by the human eye. This limitation dictates the capability of the mechanism. In order to see farther and faster, human beings rely on technological advancements. Technological advancements are a pivotal component of human progression and the evolution of the universe. When natural evolution fails to supply humanity with enhanced features, humans supplement this deficiency by using technology to invent devices that grant advantages. The abilities of the human mind mimic the role of natural evolution by providing humanity with devices that expand human potential. This allows humans to master a multitude of domains, thereby accelerating their progression along a plotted path of development.

There is an explicit demarcation between what the physical body can provide and what technological advances can create in order to extend the body's capabilities. Technology creates less dependence upon the human body toward adapting to unfamiliar environments. The evolution of the human body is not required when technological advancements supplement the body's deficiencies. Natural evolution becomes less of a necessity as the human mind develops advantages that evolution cannot contend with. The development of the mind is a subsequent phase of human progression, which eclipses advances produced by natural evolution. The progress of man does not include the transformation of the body by means of evolution; rather, the advancement of the species is enabled through the use of technology. The momentum initiated by technology has exceeded the pace set by natural evolution, when concerning the transformation of the species. As the dependency of natural evolution diminishes, its effect on humanity subsides. Positive Oppertunism transforms a species in order to give it an advantage over other species. A creature with an advantage flourishes, thereby increasing in number and enabling it to gather more resources required for its survival. As technology prevails, advantages are invented that allow humans to acquire more resources. Technology gives a human an advantage over another, thereby negating any advantage that natural evolution can provide. With the mind supplementing humanity with advantages, evolution stagnates and becomes less of an influence. Evolution is no longer required as technology satisfies the exacting demands for perfecting the human race. As necessities arise for the modification of the human body, technology is quicker to respond to correct imperfections. The age of evolution transforming the body comes to a close as a new era of divine intervention by man begins.

The role of natural evolution becomes irrelevant as the human species becomes more technologically advanced. Societies do not need to build immunities against diseases, as medicines repel bacteria. Humans can run faster as the genetic coding of individuals is modified to improve athleticism. Like an unneeded appendage, evolution wilts in the face of technological achievements. The conception of man has introduced a new variable in the transformation of existence, one that can overpower the underlying force that is changing the universe. The era of nature relying on a cryptic force to wield the path of existence is quickly diminishing. The era of man will usher in a period of divine transformation where humans dictate the change of nature and ultimately the universe. The universe is susceptible to this new form of human evolution, as humans conduct change in the universe at a faster pace. The subsequent wave of momentous change in the universe will come from humanity. Technology will replace evolution for humanity and the universe.

As humanity takes control of its own demise, the potential of man becomes limitless. The lagging evolutionary pace set by the universe no longer dictates the path of humanity. The optimization of the human body will be achieved quicker with technology than by natural evolution. The ability of humans to tap into the potential of the entire brain will be of their own doing and not that of natural evolution. As technology gains momentum, humanity will begin to set the pace for existence. The next phase of momentous change in the universe has taken hold with the introduction of humanity. □┼╫ Man has eclipsed evolution and has become the master of his evolving destiny.

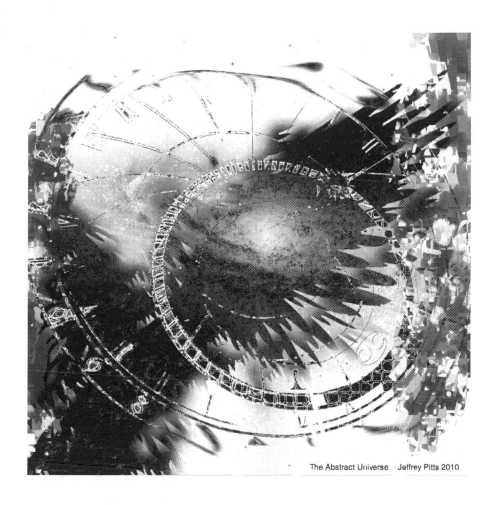

The Abstract Universe - Jeffrey Pitts 2010

Part 3 The Abstract Universe

"We are just an advanced breed of monkeys on a minor planet of a very average star. But we can understand the Universe. That makes us something very special."

Stephen Hawking (1942 -), Der Spiegel, 1989

The universe is an intricate device with many moving parts designed for a single cause. This underlying cause was fabricated as a result of its creation, and all other causes that have followed support this underlying purpose. Each component within the universe plays a role and has a purpose. Each part has been refined into an intricate component aimed at performing a specific function.

3.1 Subject Keys

Choose your path. Read key statements for every topic and mark those topics of most interest. The subject keys that appeal to you reveal insights into your human nature. Read your selections one after another, then move forward to part 4 to discover insights into your nature and how your selections reflect upon you.

KEY STATEMENT	pg
▣ Time is relative to the subject encountering it, as time is a device that ○ conforms to the convictions of its subject. Time is a measurement of change	145
▣ The default speed limit is a characteristic of the fabric of space and is ○ a component from the founding medium of existence. The heartbeat of existence	146
▣ Controlling light requires a gravitation force strong enough to blend ○ light back towards our direction. Spinning the medium of light	147
▣ ○ Existence is running on a reel at the speed of light. Slices of time	149
▣ The critical formula required to calculate future and past events ○ exists in the underlying coding of the universe. Events are predictable	151
▣ Humanity exists in a universe of ones and zeros where the outcomes ○ of events are black and white and never in between. The illusion of probability	153
▣ Determining earth's recipe provides insights into the resources ○ required to assemble such a feat. The perfect planet	155
▣ Existence is trapped in a fishbowl limited to the contents between its ○ glass walls. The limited universe	156
▣ The outward expanding edge of the universe is all-encompassing ○ and contains fields expanding at the speed of light. Boundaries of the universe	158
▣ The universe exists upon a hierarchy of mediums which govern the ○ physical laws of the universe. Laws with no bounds	159
▣ The universe can sustain itself within the void, retaining its form by ○ means of the forces operating within it. The self-sustaining universe	163

Secrets of time

Time Is a Measurement of Change

Matter is caught in a constant cycle of degradation and regeneration. It undergoes constant change, and time is used as a measure for this change. Existence is ticking away at a rate dictated by the laws of the universe. All things change at a certain pace, and the pace governing these changes cycles at unique intervals, given the function of the component in relation to the universe. Matter experiences time, but not all matter has identical experiences with time. Time becomes subjective to the component experiencing it.

Time represents something unique to each individual. Although the function of time is universally understood, its notion takes on different meanings in the modern world. Time is not a tangible item nor can it be held, so the experience of time is subjective. What you and I feel about time is different simply because we are two different things. The concept of time varies in relation to the matter experiencing it. Time acquires meaning when humans relate it to the physical world. For example, some television shows start at "prime time." Office work starts at exactly 9:00 AM and ends at 5:00 PM. It takes thirty minutes for a chicken to cook in the oven. These references give time meaning to an individual and justify its twenty-four-hour structure. ☐⊢╫ Time is relative to the subject encountering it, as time is a device that conforms to the convictions of its subject.

Humanity's perception of time is subjective, as time conforms to accommodate human life. Human time is based on phases of the Earth revolving around the Sun, creating a twenty-four-hour day. Hours and minutes can be broken down into seconds and milliseconds. Slices of time for humanity are limited to a convenient measurement conditioned on the human experience. Reality makes more sense to humans when time is divided into twenty-four-hour segments. The concept of segmented time suits humanity as it corresponds to Earth's relationship with the Sun.

Although rational, humanity's concept of time is anomalous in relation to the universe and other matter. The hours of a clock are conditioned only for humans. Other matter on Earth is not subjected to these increments, nor does it exist within the same time frame. Plants and animals do not adhere to a twenty-four-hour time interval. Creatures with limited life spans experience other segments of time. The constant attempt of quantifying the natural world with a twenty-four-hour time interval has proven unsuccessful. Humans have been trying to encapsulate the physical world within a time system that has little relation to the physical world. The process of understanding the universe gets obscured when perceiving reality through the concept of "human time." The only creatures suited for these conditioned segments of time are humans.

The Heartbeat of Existence

Objects with mass slog through space, therein disturbing other substances in their wake. Objects with no mass pose no resistance to other objects and move freely in space. Massless objects travel with no restrictions but do not travel at infinite speeds. Protons, massless particles of light, should conceptually travel at infinite speeds but rather adhere to a limit. There are underlying forces regulating all things within the universe. An invisible heartbeat exists throughout the universe, regulating the maximum allowable speed of elements. This unavoidable pace is comprised of underlying principles that govern the universe, which provide substance to the constituents that exist within them. Particles traveling at infinite speeds cannot be experienced within existence. The limiting pace with existence pauses particles long enough for existence to encounter them. Elements that logically could travel at infinite speeds adhere to this unavoidable pace of existence.

Particles traveling at the maximum allowable speed limit share commonalities with other particles with similar velocities. Those elements that adhere to this underlying limit are classified within a unique category. The default speed limit is imposed upon those elements, which have no boundaries on speed. Those elements with the capacity to travel at boundless speeds are confined by an invisible force. □┤╫ The default speed limit is a characteristic of the fabric of space and is a component from the founding medium of existence. The medium of existence regulates the absolute increment of time, as no other increment of time can be devised from it. The maximum speed of change equates to an instance of existence as regulated by the underlying medium of the universe.

The default speed limit acts like a movie camera projector, regulating the pace of film and images passing through it. It limits the rate at which each frame can be projected. Objects can zip past the movie image scene but cannot travel faster than the speed in which the projector can turn the reel. Objects moving quickly across the screen move slower than the frame rate of the projector, or else they will not be seen. Elements found in this classification share a unique relationship as each particle influences the other of equal vector value and not greater. The rate of existence dictates the pace of light, which bonds those who experience light with the fixed heartbeat of the universe.

Spinning the Medium of Light

Light is a phenomenon. Humans utilize light to perceive events as they happen. We are certain that events occur when we perceive them firsthand. Out of the five senses, sight retrieves information the quickest through light. For example, in a lightning storm we perceive the lightning spectacle prior to hearing the trailing thunder sound. Light is abundant throughout the universe. Humans use light to perceive the farthest galaxies in the universe. Light plays a critical role in existence as it is the primary conveyer of human experiences. Events that occurred in life, first occurred in light.

Perceiving the past is a process that involves the collection of historical light. Astronomers practice this technique when they peer into the night sky and observe ancient starlight. Stars appearing in the sky are a reminiscent of their current state. Light traveling to Earth from the stars is aged, thereby displaying historical glimpses into the universe. By the time the light from stars reaches the Earth, it is dated. Astronomers have been able to perceive the light emanating since the beginning of time. The night sky becomes a window into the past, displaying historical events within the cosmos.

Humans experience the physical universe using senses, but heavily depend upon light to experience the past. Light reflects current and historical events like those found through radio broadcasts in space. Light is the medium that carries these experiences, similar to the film on a movie reel. If we could retrieve that light, we would be able to see a window into Earth's past. The retrieval of historic light involves the process of reflecting or warping radiated waves of light. A remnant of this radiated light exists in space and must be captured in order to be perceived. Capturing light in a bottle is an old fable that is scientifically impossible. Alternatives to capturing light involve controlling its direction. ▯⊢⊪ Controlling light requires a gravitation force strong enough to bend light back toward our direction. The objective is to manipulate the path of light through the use of gravity. Radiating light could be bent and spun, and therefore could be stored. A gravity well could hold the history of the universe in the form of captured light. Historical events projected years ago would return for us to view. Viewing historical events would be as easy as turning on a television.

Slices of Time

Change occurs in increments. The rate of change is measured in time. An instance of time is the smallest increment of change that can occur. It is the smallest increment in which one particle can move from one location to another. This increment represents a slice or frame of existence. An instance of time is a snapshot of one frame of existence. A snapshot captures all elements in a nonmoving state, where every element is perfectly still. Elements appearing in the snapshot cannot travel quicker than one instance of captured time. Every snapshot displays nonmoving objects, although in reality they may be moving at extreme velocities. Several snapshots flipped together create the re-enactment of elements in motion.

Human life consists of several slices of time spliced together. The amalgamation of the slices equates to existence, an experiential picture show sequenced with time. Although your experiential slices differ from another person's, they both comply with the same rate and frequency. They both comply with the universal rate of existence that has been imposed by the principles governing existence. Slices of time occur at an identical rate on the other side of the universe as they do on Earth. Existence is bound to a steady inescapable rate of time.

The rate of time is measured in increments, which equates to one instance of light per frame of existence. Light exists on a medium that dictates the pace at which existence adheres to. Each frame of light represents one frame of existence. Light is the oil that paints the canvas of existence and illuminates each sequence of existence. The maximum rate of change occurs at the speed of light. The conception of time began at the first change of existence, which occurred at the speed of light. The beginning of time and the Big Bang are synonymous, during which existence adhered to an underlying frame rate that defined experience. ⊡⊣⊦⊦ Existence is running on a reel at the speed of light.

3.3 *The Scripted Universe*

> *"There is a theory which states that if ever anybody discovers exactly what the Universe is for and why it is here, it will instantly disappear and be replaced by something even more bizarre and inexplicable. There is another theory which states that this has already happened."*
>
> Douglas Adams (1952 - 2001)

Events are Predictable

Time travel is a popular subject in science fiction. The concept of traveling to any point backward or forward in time conjures endless possibilities of discoveries and mystery solving. The common perception of time travel entails placing a human in a device and moving the device at speeds faster than light. More so, this process will transfer the individual to another time, leaving the individual unharmed inside the device. Present-day science is unable to construct such a device, nor fathom how it could be built. There are several obstacles deterring humanity from accomplishing such a feat. The process of time travel is not forgiving to matter, as elements of substance deteriorate with accelerated speeds. Matter tends to be the obstacle preventing an object from moving through time. As human beings are composed of matter, the possibilities of time travel dampens, but the concept of time travel does not limit itself to what you can physically experience. If you have the ability to predict the future, then you share a quality with the time traveler. Predicting the future with precision solely based on calculations allows you to see the future without moving matter. Science entails predicting future events using proven methods. Science uses simple formulas to calculate probable outcomes. The ability of predicting the future with precision also suggests the ability to decipher the past. Calculating past and future events based on current variables provides a tangible method for understanding and experiencing alternate periods of time. To put this into perspective, consider the following scenario. With the known laws of physics, throwing a ball high up in the air will result in the ball's return at the same velocity. Scientific principles determine the speed of the returning ball and the amount of time it would take to return. The future projection of the ball has been predicted, which complies with the formulas of physics. Now if a ball from the sky were to hit you on top of your head, science could decipher where it came from and at which time the ball was dropped. Therefore, the past movement of the ball could be deciphered. This scenario illustrates a simple example of predicting the past and future. Science is the time machine, using proven formulas to calculate precise outcomes in reality.

Pieces of the universe are revealed once you are able to determine events prior to them happening. In the same breath, you can understand historical events with the variables that exist in the present day. Scientists predict outcomes of experiments based on controlled variables and environments. As existence becomes more understood, the understanding of our environment becomes more controlled, allowing us to comprehend complicated variables. The variables involved in calculating future events are currently beyond human comprehension but are more understood with the advancement of knowledge. The critical component for predicting future events lies in knowing the ultimate algorithm of existence and injecting present-day variables into this algorithm. ☐┤╫ The critical formula required to calculate future and past events exists in the underlying coding of the universe. The primary code of the universe is the basis for predicting past and future events. With the proper inputs, this mathematical equation would produce a precise outcome of any event, at any time. By manipulating a time variable, we can calculate the position, event, and state of any event. These calculations will open a window into the past and future, where humanity could forward or rewind existence. With the universe being so complex, the ability to perceive past and future events will not be claimed for some time.

The Illusion of Probability

Humanity is surrounded by an ambiguous existence of probabilities. We are uncertain of everything because popular science pronounces that we live in a statistical world where probabilities dictate events. This perception gives rise to uncertainty, which fuels the illusion of reality. Reality feels better when it is conditioned upon chance. The concept that events happen by chance gives rise to luck and randomness. It promotes the opportunity of endless possibilities and boundaries. Things that cannot be explained are often associated with chance. Humans accommodate themselves when describing an event in reality as a random occurrence.

Everything in existence is predictable. We label events as random because understanding the outcome of an event requires knowledge beyond current human comprehension. Because variables for a given event are too vast to comprehend, it is easier to claim that events occurred because of chance. A controlled experiment in a controlled environment produces consistent results. Understanding and controlling each variable in a controlled experiment yields consistent results. Non-controlled environments contain uncertain variables that exceed comprehension, so humanity generalizes such events, labelling them as random occurrences. The use of generalizations gives rise to probabilities. Probabilities are statistical estimates, calculated to approximate probable outcomes for events. The process of probability is a deficiency of certainty allowing for chance to participate in calculated outcomes. The inability to comprehend the science behind an event with certainty is a human deficiency that is supplemented with convenient equations of probability. As humanity progresses, certain theories are put into place to explain the unexplainable out of convenience. For instance, consider viewing an image of a tropical landscape on the television screen. From a distance, we see images of the swaying trees portrayed on the screen, but from up close, the tree images become a series of colored dots that form the image. It is easier to describe the image on the screen rather than the individual dots displayed. The inability to describe the thousands of dots gives rise to a convenient description of the image.

The universe is composed of calculative events that yield certain results every time. The likelihood of some event happening over another is nonexistent, as each event is certain to happen always. The degree of some event turning out this way or that way will vary, but the outcome is always certain. ⬜—⫲ Humanity exists in a universe of ones and zeros, where the outcomes of events are black and white, and never in between. This concept provides the foundation of certainty and gives rise to humanity's destiny as being scripted. The probability of events leading to humanity's demise is clearly defined in a calculation. Removing the lingering component of time from the equation will concede all events and consolidate humanity into its scripted demise. Time is the catalyst that prolongs the outcome of a preconceived existence. Without time, the product calculated from events in existence would produce specified results instantly.

The Limits of the Universe

> *"Only two things are infinite, the universe and human stupidity, and I'm not sure about the former."*
>
> Albert Einstein (1879 - 1955)

The Perfect Planet

Successful recipes require specific amounts of ingredients and precise instructions. The Earth is a successful recipe consisting of the right combination of elements for the creation of life. The correct balance of elements has given rise to an Eden located in barren space. The correct combination of elements have wound together to form a hospitable planet where the inevitability of life was certain. The precise collection of elements from various stars and planets combined to form life on Earth.

The ingredients required to create life on Earth did not originate from one solar system, galaxy, or cluster, but rather from several. Determining the number of systems partaking in Earth's creation provides an understanding in the fundamental requirements and magnitude involved in creating such a scheme. Understanding where the ingredients originated from creates a chain of events leading back to the initial point of Earth's assembly. □─┼┤ Determining Earth's recipe provides insights into the resources required to assemble such a feat. The magnitude of production provides information on other possible Earth-like planets in the universe. Key measurements involved in the process would have to be identified, including the amount of time, space, resources, and quantified mixing of material required to create an Earth and only one Earth. The abundance of resources required for such a task would have come from an exclusive portion of the universe dedicated to the formation of an Earth. If the quantity of the universe required to make the Earth is one fourth its total size, then the probability of making another Earth can only exist in the other three-fourths portion. Given this scenario, there are enough resources for the production of three more Earths in the entire universe. Those other Earths would then have a Sun, Moon, and solar system similar to Earth. The participants on these planets would navigate using the stars as guides following the constellation, as humans do.

In order to create a hospitable environment for humanity, the limiting boundaries of planet Earth would not suffice. The amount of space required for a species like humans go beyond Earth's solar system, cluster, and galaxy. The limits extend beyond the farthest physical reaches known to man. The environment's capacity has to accommodate the experiential spectrum capable of man. Humanity requires a testing ground of a certain size to grow in and experiment. Impingement of these resources within the required boundaries would limit humanity's capacity to develop into their ultimate potential. Every star we see in the sky accommodates humanity, as they are required to entertain human potential. The universe has to reserve the appropriate size of space for humanity in order to allow the human mental capacity to flourish. The capacity of the human mind is endless, making the universe's tasks of accommodating such a creature difficult.

The Limited Universe

The physical universe has limitations. Everything that is susceptible to change is finite in quantity. Matter, like anything that you can hold in your hand, has limitations. Matter cannot be infinite, travel at unlimited speeds, have an infinite size, have infinite density, or be indivisible indefinitely, and it cannot contain infinite energy. □⊢Ⅲ Existence is trapped in a fishbowl limited to the contents between its glass walls. Humanity has been given a fixed amount of clay that it can mold and work with.

Figure 16   Limited Matter

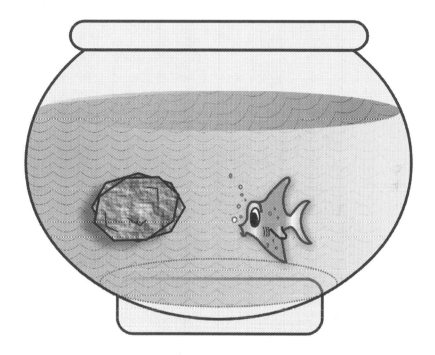

Matter does not grow on trees, from a physicist's perspective. We all know that the Earth grows and accumulates more dirt on its crust every year, but it does not increase in weight. Aside from the several meteorites that slam into Earth's surface, the Earth does not add any weight to its initial mass. Although the Earth is transforming, its initial weigh has not experienced any monumental shift. The Earth is solitarily confined, able to transform but within its own means of mass. The matter comprising the Earth has transformed but has not increased or decreased in quantity. This utopian dilemma is a microcosm of the universe. Matter tends to clump due to the predominant force of gravity, but the weight collected within a clump is not newfound mass; rather, the mass had always existed. The universe has a potential mass that it cannot exceed. This limit is based on the initial energy housed within the universe. For every portion of energy, there is a potential of mass and no more. Physical matter and energy have a limit in a limited universe. Figure 16 depicts the limited matter within a fishbowl existence.

Boundaries of the Universe

Voyaging beyond the limits of the universe requires traveling beyond the speed of light. Outside the universe is an infinite void with no sound or light, where sensory experiences cease to exist. An individual floating in the void would be in a dream-like state, where only the mind and thought would subsist. Experiential sensorium would arrive when the first wave of fields expanding the universe would come rushing by. The first wave of light would appear and then the sensation of weight from other objects in the universe would be felt. This is the point where the edge of the universe begins, where fields populate the void and expand space. ⬜⊢⊪ The outward expanding edge of the universe is all-encompassing and contains fields expanding at the speed of light.

Every limiting portion of the universe is connected together by interacting fields. The universe is filled with fields that bounce and interact with each other. Those fields traveling at the greatest of speeds are the elements heading the expansion of space itself. Fields encroach upon the limits of the universe expanding it, as they are the elements that travel with the greatest velocities. The expansion of the universe occurs within a consolidated sphere of fields. This draws a clear demarcation between the universe's boundary and the void beyond its limits. The territories encroached by expanding fields still adhere to the physical principles governing the rest of the universe. The fields expand upon a canvas regulated by the laws that govern reality. The blank canvas or void could be considered as an unlimited barren territory waiting to be populated.

As the universe inflates into unknown territory, it expands and enlarges its internal volume. The potency and solidarity of matter and fields become stretched and loose, as the integrity of the universe diminishes. The larger the universe expands, the more gaps manifest between substances. The push of matter from the point of creation diminishes the interaction between elements within the universe. The farther one element is from another, the less likely those elements will influence each other. The outcome of continuous expansion leads to elements becoming isolated and detached from the collectiveness of the universe. A universe without relationships becomes stagnant and bleak.

Laws with No Bounds

The creation of matter was an evolutionary feat designed to capture energy. Matter is a by-product produced by the interaction of energy and universal fields. Matter is defined by the resistance it imposes upon universal fields. This resistance endows matter with mass, weight, and inevitably a gravitational field. The principles governing the weight of matter are derived from underlying mediums that dictate its behavior in the physical universe. Matter exists within several mediums that give it substance. Those mediums beyond matter's initial medium work in unison, providing substance to matter. The universe is a collaboration of mediums supporting substances within it. These mediums are the building blocks of elements found within the universe. The relationship between matter and its mediums is critical in understanding matter's function and workings in the universe.

⬚┼╟ The universe exists upon a hierarchy of mediums that govern the physical laws of the universe. This hierarchy consists of several mediums that rely upon one another, forming a platform for existence to dwell on. Underlying mediums situated at the bottom of the hierarchy support those mediums above them. This chain of support continues throughout the mediums and onto matter that sits upon them. Physical elements in the universe require a medium in order to exist, similar to the relationship a fish has with water. The fish requires water to survive, but the water alone does not make the fish exist. The fish is influenced by several mediums that give substance to it and the water. The molecules composing the fish and water need substance, which are provided by sequential mediums. A chain of reliance continues until the underlying medium of existence is reached. The underlying medium relies upon itself and is the founding structure of the universe. This medium is balanced upon itself, relying on opposing forces to maintain its cohesion. The combination of mediums influence elements within the universe and give substance to elements. The layering of mediums dictate the physical laws that manipulate elements within the universe.

Mediums are composed of matter, fields, energy, and so on. Those mediums that are in direct contact with an element are labelled as *direct mediums* and have a greater effect over those distant mediums lower on the hierarchy. Direct mediums located on top of the hierarchy highly influence an element compared to the minimal influences conveyed by *indirect mediums* nearing the bottom of the hierarchy. Mediums composed of matter take precedence over those composed of fields. Physical mediums are regulated by underlying mediums, which dictate the physical principles of matter. The layering of mediums dictates the actions of those mediums higher on the hierarchy. Layered mediums are like the layers of a cake where the bottom layers influence the structure of the top layers.

Several underlying mediums exist within other dimensions. Their influences are negligible compared to direct mediums, but their influences are felt more uniformly throughout the universe. The layering of mediums within layered dimensions builds upon principles governing elements within the universe. Each medium creates another principle that regulates how physical elements interact in the universe. Figure 17 displays the hierarchy of dimensional mediums influencing the universe. Medium 230 is defined by the mediums layered within the last four dimensions (D1 to D4). Mediums located in the universe retain values present in mediums located in other dimensions. Medium M92 is located in dimension four (D4) and is the amalgamation of mediums M12, M15, M22, M23, and M43.

Figure 17   Layered Dimensions and Mediums

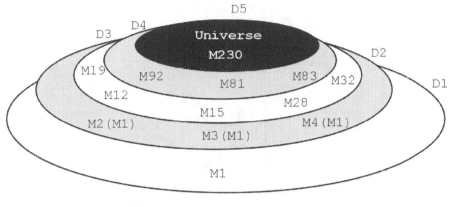

D = Dimensions
M12= [M3(M1),M5(M1)]
M15= [M3(M1), M2(M1)]
M92= (M12, M15, M22, M23, M43)
M230= (M92, M81, M83)

Mediums define the overall shape and size of elements under their influence. The size and shape of the universe is restricted and defined by its mediums. The universe is expanding at a rate dictated by its medium. Figure 18 displays the relationship between mediums and the expanding universe. Areas with substance are represented by the rings on the diagram, which illustrate the layering of mediums. Matter and fields are inflating, radiating outwardly, and compose the edges of the universe (E). The universe is expanding at the speed of light on mediums regulating physical principles.

Figure 18

Mediums of the Universe

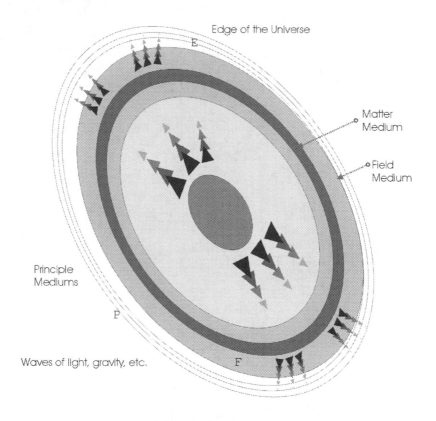

Edge of the Universe

E

Matter
Medium

Field
Medium

Principle
Mediums

P

Waves of light, gravity, etc.

F

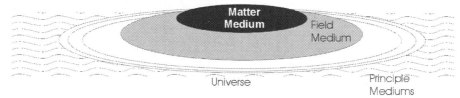

Matter
Medium

Field
Medium

Universe

Principle
Mediums

The Self-Sustaining Universe

The universe rests on a desolate void, an infinite plateau of nothingness suspended onto itself. Something existing in nothingness does not drop or fall, make a sound, or interact, it just exists. The void surrounding the universe is not trying to break it apart nor compress it together. The only force imposed on the universe is within the universe itself. The universe has the capability to implode or explode. It is free to exercise either of these actions as the void does not impose restrictions. The universe is the force forging its own demise. The universe is dictating its shape and growth, a free-wielding entity subject to its own limitations. The universe is growing and expanding, populating the void or nothingness at its own pace. When nothingness gets populated, it becomes something, and that initial something is space. Space is something, a conductor of fields, energy, and matter. The medium of space houses elements that the universe can experience. Space is expanding and, in the process of stretching, creates a negative pressure on substances within it. The relationship between space and matter is limited by the physical principles that govern their behavior. Matter has no special privileges in relation to space, as it acts the same anywhere in space, adhering to the same physical laws. Conflicting forces are at work between space and matter, as matter is constantly at work, clumping and gouging divots into space, while space wants to disperse matter and prevent it from clumping, thereby retaining a flat, uniform shape. It is the struggle between these two elements that cause the promotion of motion and change.

Matter congeals in order to counteract the inflation of space. If enough matter groups together, the force of gravity keeps the matter solidified, resisting the separating force of space. The matter becomes self-sustained and creates a divot in the fabric of space. Figure 19 displays portions of matter carved into the fabric of space. The force of gravity pushes through the fabric of space while the fabric expands, forcing the matter out from its hole. The matter is not separating, sliding, falling, or slipping in space. The forces of gravity solidify and unite the clump, balancing out retracting forces that infringe on its solidity.

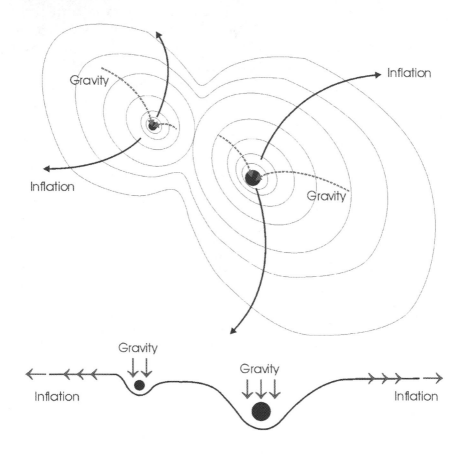

Figure 19   Self-Containing Universe

The forces of push and pull constantly influence matter in space, similar to a ball suspended in water, as displayed in Figure 20. A ball is suspended in a tank of water with gravity pulling the ball downward and buoyancy forcing the ball upward. The ball's weight is perfectly balanced, allowing it to be suspended in the center of the tank, thereby not allowing either of the forces to overwhelm it. Just like the ball, the conglomeration of matter and fields that form the universe are self-sustaining. This self-sustaining property reinforces the universe's cohesion, not allowing it to disperse or implode. ▢┼╫ The universe can sustain itself within the void, retaining its form by means of the forces operating within it. The universe is balanced between two forces of inflation and retraction, although inflation is exerting a greater force than retraction. The universe succumbs to the expanding force of inflation, although both forces of inflation and retraction are near the same intensity. The universe is able to sustain itself by not completely succumbing to either of the forces, thereby balancing out the forces of retraction and inflation. Figure 21 displays the relationship between the push and pull of matter. As dark matter congeals, creating a stronger gravitational attraction force (Point B) at the center of the universe, the inflationary repulsion force (Point C) repels matter, neutralizing the overwhelming influence of either force. As the universe expands upon the blank plateau (Point D), it maintains its rigidity through its internal forces of attraction and repulsion, thereby making it self-sustaining within void.

| Figure 20 | Suspended Universe |

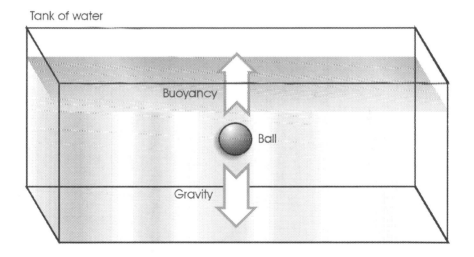

Tank of water

Buoyancy

Ball

Gravity

Figure 21   Balanced Universe

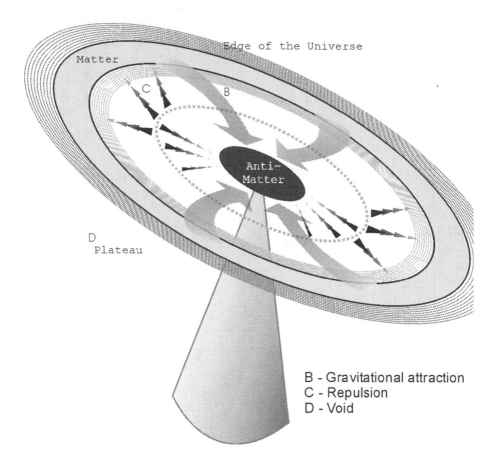

Edge of the Universe

Matter

C

B

Anti-
Matter

D
Plateau

B - Gravitational attraction
C - Repulsion
D - Void

The 21ˢᵗ Century Paradigm

> *"Your paradigm is so intrinsic to your mental process that you are hardly aware of its existence, until you try to communicate with someone with a different paradigm."*
>
> Donella Meadows, The Global Citizen

Acceptance of Universal Laws

The concept of time is subjective in relation to humanity, as it represents different things for different experiences. An insect's concept of time is experientially different from another creature's. Similarly, human time is experientially different from the universe's time. As time is experienced relatively, a universal concept of time is unrealistic. The concept of a universal time system is difficult to construct because reality is more compatible with a subjective system. Humans are comfortable with a subjective time system that suits their experiential existence. A universal time system would be applicable to humanity when conditions become suitable for the species.

In order to quantify the disorderly universe, humanity constructs rules for reality. These rules measure and justify experiences. The world and substances within the universe are subject to these rules, thereby allowing humanity to make sense of its obscured environment. Humanity's progression, in relation to its environment, follows certain prescribed rules that contort reality into a digestible form. Man's existence is subject to his environmental circumstances and should not be regulated by circumstances outside his experience. ☐⊢Ⅲ Experiential rules formulated by humans comply with their immediate environment and not those foreign to them or beyond their scope. As humanity progresses, the boundaries of its environment increase, thereby introducing new rules and experiential laws. As humanity gazes closer at the stars and travels farther out into space, man moves closer to laws and rules that govern the universe. As humanity's environment expands, it adheres to universal absolutes and principles for daily living, thereby gradually adopting universal laws into daily activities. The average comprehension of the experiential world increases, resulting in the acceptance of universal principles for quantifying daily routines. Humanity faces scientific thresholds where existing scientific policies need to conform to new scientific policies in order to suit new circumstances. With advancements in human progression, the willingness to conform to subsequent rules becomes overwhelming and unanimous. A paradigm shift ensues, complementing the reformed human condition.

Existence is governed by physical laws that dictate the interaction of elements. These universal truths have been uncovered by science. Experiments are conducted to prove theories, but there are some theories that are simply based on logic; they cannot be proven. Principles that are proven through experiments are readily accepted by scientists, but theories with no experiential evidence are rarely accepted. Proving a theory through experiment validates a concept as being applicable in reality and to the current condition of humanity's technological capabilities. Conceptual theories that prove logical but lack experiential evidence are held with uncertainty. Logical concepts that exist outside the realm of human experience receive less attention and validation, because the concepts lie outside the human experimental scope. They are less applicable to reality and therefore are generalized as plausible concepts in search of experiential evidence. For instance, watching an image of swaying trees on a television concisely summarizes the objects until one moves closer to the television to realize that the images are a combination of colored dots grouped to produce the image. Until that time of experiential realization, the concept of the image being a conglomeration of dots becomes a plausible concept. The theory is placed on idle, waiting for evidence to allow the general public to comply with the concept. Without the ability to see the dots, the concept of the image being composed of them becomes less readily accepted. Universal laws that govern the universe outside the realm of humanity's experience are not readily adopted as rules that govern humanity. Humans are less readily willing to accept concepts that do not pertain to their perceived realities.

The success of theoretical concepts are weighed upon their relevance to the application. Humanity will gradually adopt universe truths as mainstream principles when human progression advances toward conditions in which humanity is forced to accept a more relevant application. Humanity's willingness to adopt these universal laws becomes evident as it reconnects itself as a component of the universe. As humanity's environment expands and advances to regions outside the Earth, the concepts of universal principles will gain more relevance and become staples of human living. These principles will be integrated into human reality as their relevance becomes more substantial. With human perceptions expanding, humanity will adopt these universal concepts when they apply to the immediate reality.

Reality Is an Illusion

Perceptions, like preferences, differ among individuals. The complexity of the mind conditions individuals to perceive reality uniquely. Reality is relative, as experiences differ between individuals. Everything in existence is viewed through individual perspectives, and no one thing can be certain in the experiential world. Like the uniqueness of the pattern of a snowflake, one perception will vary from another indefinitely. Reality suddenly becomes subjective and uncertain. The application of logic is applied to reality to delude its illusion. □—⫴ The progression of humanity entails dissolving the illusion of reality through the advancement of knowledge. It is the mission of science to quantify individual experiences into predictable calculations.

The changing world becomes challenging to define through individual perspectives. Defining reality requires developing a consensus between several perspectives. The popular consensus becomes the definition of reality and establishes a foothold over other possible perspectives. A mutual consensus is recognized, which eliminates other subjective influences from other individual perceptions, thereby establishing a universal viewpoint. This viewpoint is perceived without bias as being true everywhere in existence. A portrait of reality is created, distilling the bewilderment of reality's illusion. As humans progress, they follow consensus to define reality. Perspectives accepted as fact retain some form of credibility, guiding humanity toward legitimizing reality. The definitions of reality accommodate the people following them, serving a purpose for the one thing that is certain: the mind.

What is certain about the experiential world is that it is uncertain. Things that can be experienced are the substances masking the logic behind the illusion of reality. To understand existence is to understand the puppeteer behind the illusion. Experiential events susceptible to subjective perspectives cannot be perceived with certainty. The experiential world becomes an illusion, as there is no sense in what is definitively real. Humans exist in an elaborate illusion governed by logical principles manipulating experiential things. The illusion portrays an experiential playground for humanity to experiment in. At a point in human maturity, the playground will dissolve and the true underlying fabric of the universe will be revealed. The methods of escaping the confines of relativity are through the means of logical thought. Logical thought extends beyond the experiential world and identifies the puppeteer.

Reality Redefined

The only thoughts we can be certain to exist are our own, as reality is certain to exist only to ourselves. The universe toils in relation to one individual: ourselves. Logic supports the conclusion that the universe does not revolve around one individual, as there are grander schemes in the universe that supersede one individual's experience. These schemes consist of universal truths and, like our thoughts, supersede reality. Universal truths, like physical principles, hold true to all things that happen over here or over there. They are the laws and foundation upon which reality exists and are not subject to manipulation but rather exert their influence upon reality. They are the primary functions that have founded the universe and are known to be true even during the conception of existence. The laws that govern the universe exist outside the confines of the universe, manipulating elements within it. They are the principles that have founded the primordial coding of the universe.

The universe is structured upon multiple segments of cryptic code, like a complicated jigsaw puzzle. Deciphering the code is like putting the pieces of the puzzle together. The scattered pieces of the puzzle are universal truths required for understanding the picture of the universe. Universal truths create a foundation for the coding of the universe. The formulation containing the makings of the universe is structured on universal truths. The answers about everything lie in these truths and not in the picture show we are uncertain to experience in reality. These truths sustain the coding of the universe and describe everything that is beyond the individual perspective. The gradual discovery of these truths will bring humanity closer to understanding the universe's code. The progression of humanity involves the acquisition of knowledge pertaining to these universal truths.

Things we cannot touch or experience, but are known to exist, are conceptualized with science. Science builds theories on how things function in the universe. These theories are filled with mathematical principles, which plot sequential movements and actions within the cosmos. The process of discovering these principles is similar to the workings of a detective at a crime scene. A detective maps out the crime scene to unlock the pattern of events that have led to the crime. Evidence found at the crime scene points out a distinct trail of sequential events. Explaining how events came to be requires detective work, but explaining how things came about in the universe sometimes extends beyond human comprehension. More often we don't have the knowledge or the tools to identify the evidence. For example, the world was once considered to be the center of the universe; it was thought that everything revolved around the Earth. A functional working model was developed of the cosmos in relation to the Earth at its center, and it was reasonably sound but not practical. Although the model explained the detailed sequence of the planets turning in the sky, the model had minor inconsistencies. It wasn't until an unlikely fisherman presented a more practical model, with the Sun presiding at the center of the solar system, that the correct model was discovered. The hypothesis was correct and brought practicality to the cosmos. The first model could have easily passed as the truth because although complex, it correctly showed the sequence of the Sun traveling past the Earth. Although the first model was incorrect, it was suitable to the human application until another more plausible theory was developed. The first model fit its time until its glaring inconsistencies could no longer be dismissed and a new model was introduced. This conundrum is present today as humanity defines its world in relation to its current progressive maturity. As knowledge is accumulated, the way humanity defines existence will seem impractical to future generations. Humanity is constantly poised for the introduction of new theories defining existence. Finding the answers that define the universe will require examining evidence in order to solve the mystery.

Humanity easily dismisses everything as relative due to the convenience of the theory. At its current progressive stage, humanity cannot comprehend the complexities behind the making of events occurring in reality. Reality is deemed as subjective, like a group of random events subject to chance. There are no clear answers as to why events happen in a certain way rather than in another, thereby opening the explanation of events to subjective interpretation. This conundrum annunciates that every perception of an event, although different, is potentially correct. One person may describe an event differently from another person, but each description is correct as each event is relative to that person. This may seem impractical and it is, but the model suits the human condition at its current progressive stage. ⎕—III The pieces of the puzzle defining reality are beyond human comprehension; therefore, the current impractical theories of existence become fitting for the human condition.

The founding principles that form the foundation of reality branch out into an amalgamation of conjoined principles. Founding principles connect together to create refined laws suitable for the realm they govern. As time passes, the principles continue to be refined, creating a comprehensive platform and allowing for the opportunity of complicated elements to converge. This process of principle refinement is an evolving component in the universe. Every action within the universe abides by these principles, and every motion has been defined by these principles, scripted to perform a sequence of events. All events, no matter how complex, are principles in action, one following the other in suite. These actions are not relative or subject to chance, but follow a methodical sequence of coding scripted by the principles governing existence. Events are not defined by perception, but by the accrued principles governing existence. Humanity has only discovered a fraction of these principles. A universal truth is consistent throughout the universe and cannot be defined by opinions but rather by calculations, resulting in specific conclusions. Events occurring in the universe are a result of mathematical conditions that are always known to be certain.

Finding the coordinates of the Earth within the universe is not mathematically precise. The current calculations for Earth's position are estimates, as science does not possess all the variables involved in defining the equation. Humanity can never be certain of all the variables within an equation relating to existence. Controlling the variables in an experiment allows for a conclusive prediction of the outcome. If humanity is able to define all the variables involved in an event, future outcomes would be revealed. Understanding these variables would require an understanding of the equations governing the universe. Understanding every variable within the universe would define the makings of the universe and its creator. Humanity would discover that the universe can be defined under conclusive specifications. A properly controlled experiment would reveal the same outcome for every perception. Physical existence would be defined with certainty and understanding all events throughout history would become possible.

Figure 22   Variables Leading to an Event

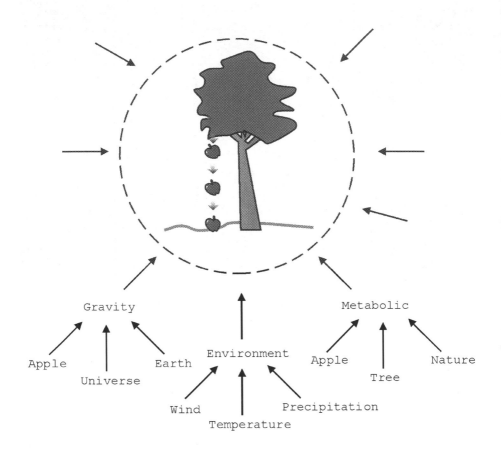

Defining the variables for events requires discovering the cause and effect of each event since the beginning of existence. As each event is governed by mathematical principles, knowing the sequence of variables for the principles will provide a conclusive result of sequential events. Figure 22 displays the hierarchical chain of events leading to an apple falling off a tree. Identifying the variables and principles involved in such an event solidifies the conclusion of the cause for the apple falling. The hierarchy of variables is too vast for human comprehension, rendering the result of the apple falling by chance. By deducing all the variables and principles since the beginning of time, the conclusion would definitely lead to an apple falling at that exact moment.

Attractive Forces

> *"We can lick gravity, but sometimes the paperwork is overwhelming."*
>
> Wernher Von Braun (1912 - 1977)

Gravity, an Accumulative Force

Gravity waves radiate with higher magnitudes when multiplied. Its field can compound when aligned, or compress when in opposing trajectories. Objects swirling in Earth's solar system are affected by multiple gravitational fields radiating from multiple objects. Objects on Earth, although pinned down by Earth's gravity, are affected by other gravitational fields in the solar system. For instance, the Moon's gravitational force regulates Earth's tides. High tide occurs when the Moon is closest to the body of water on which it exerts its influence. The compounding gravitational effects of the Moon, Sun, and other planetary objects in the solar system affect the gravitational influence Earth exerts upon objects on its surface. Figure 23 displays the hierarchy of gravity wells in Earth's solar system. The dominant Gravitational Force B caused by Object J is the primary point of gravitational influence within the universe. Its gravitational force directly influences other objects in the universe exerting lesser influence.

The proper alignment of planetary objects in Earth's solar system produces a greater gravitational pull or push upon Earth and upon objects on its surface. Humans feel lighter during an eclipse when they align themselves between the Sun, Moon, and the Earth. The combined gravitational force of the Sun and Moon are essentially pulling the objects on Earth's surface, thereby weakening Earth's gravitational influence on those objects. The opposite effect is

Figure 23 — Hierarchy of Gravity Wells

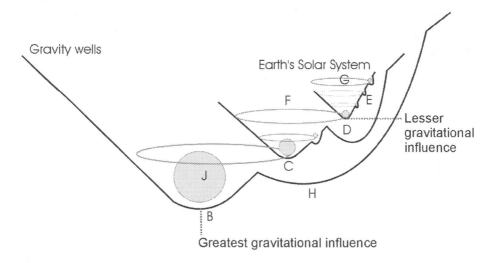

B - Dominant gravitational well
C - Subservient gravity well
D - Gravity well of the sun in Earth's solar system
E - Circular orbit of the Earth
F - Circular orbit of Earth's solar system; gravitational orbit of subservient well C
H - Gravitational imprint of subservient well C on well B
J - Heaviest object

experienced for objects on Earth's opposing side, where objects feel pulled down when enduring the accumulated gravitational force of the Sun, Moon, and Earth. This celestial alignment is forcing objects toward Earth's surface with greater strength. Figure 24 illustrates the effect of accumulative gravitational forces from two sources. The diagram displays a larger bucket (Bucket F), which is the dominant gravitational force, and a smaller bucket (Bucket B) inside the larger one, which exerts a weaker gravitational force. Bucket F is spinning in a circular motion with Bucket B spinning within it. The centrifugal forces of the buckets are increased when Bucket B is aligned with the directional centrifugal point of Bucket F. When Bucket B swings

Figure 24 — Accumulative Centrifugal Force

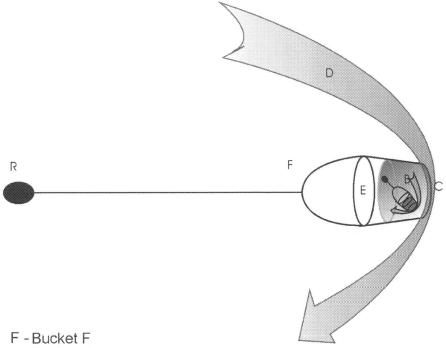

F - Bucket F
B - Bucket B
C - Strongest centrifugal force of bucket F. Point were bucket B attains the strongest accumulated force.
D - Constant circular motion of swinging bucket F
E - Point where bucket B has the least amount of accumulative centrifugal force with bucket F
R - Directional centrifugal point

toward the central point of Bucket F's centrifugal force (R), the two forces compete, and the water in Bucket B is less compressed against the bottom of the bucket. This relationship exists among the Sun, Moon, Earth, and other planetary objects that exert a gravitational influence. The constant fluctuations of gravitational influences manipulate objects on Earth, depending upon their position on the surface of Earth. Although this accumulative influence is minuscule

Figure 25 — Planetary Gravitational Pull

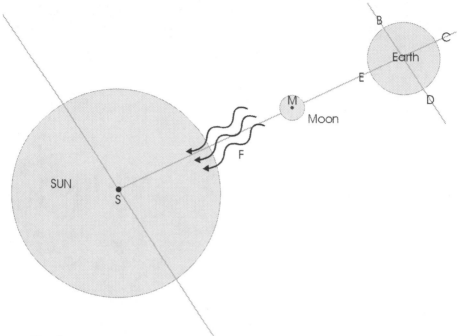

E - Greatest gravitational influence by the sun and moon, least accumulative gravitational pull from the earth

C - Least amount of gravitational influence by the sun and moon, greatest accumulative gravitational pull

F - Sun's gravitation pull direction

B/D - Constant accumulative gravitational pull

S/M - Directional centrifugal point

and not easily detected, it affects all objects of mass. ☐⊣⊩ Therefore, it would be easier for an Olympic high jumper to break the world record when aligned with the Sun and Moon during an eclipse.

Figure 25 displays the gravitational relationship among the Sun, Moon, and Earth. When Earth aligns itself with the Sun and Moon during a solar eclipse, the gravitational effects caused by the celestial objects are intensified upon objects on Earth's surface. Objects located on Earth's surface (E) are in line with the direct gravitational pull of the Sun (S) and the Moon (M). These objects will experience a lesser gravitational pull by Earth's gravitational field. Objects that are distant from Point E (Point B, C, D) will experience Earth's gravitational influence at a greater magnitude.

Resistance of Mass

Objects in the universe endure a constant struggle with external forces. To merely exist implies there is resistance as matter is continuously resisting underlying universal fields. Interaction with these forces provides definition for matter and gives it substance. Without resistance, matter would have no mass, would not clump, and could not be sensed. The underlying fields that form the foundation of the universe resist elements, resulting in the creation of matter. As elements accelerate through these fields, the interaction causes an array of effects, including providing matter with substance. The faster the elements move through these fields, the greater the resistance. The friction caused by this interaction forces elements to transform and evolve. Substance is acquired when elements transform into matter and gain a stronger gravitational field. Figure 26 displays an object accelerating through fields. The initial resisting fields (B) are uniform and show no distress, but as Object C begins to accelerate, the resisting fields become distorted (D). The massive accelerating object (Object E) causes a reaction in the fields (D), making them warp. The residual effect of this distortion gives matter substance and creates a gravitational effect. Object E attains substance when fields accelerate through Object E, causing friction. Consider a ball moving in a tank of water, as illustrated in Figure 26. The greater the velocity of the ball (H), the more turbulence (G) is generated. The calmness of the water becomes disturbed, and the residual effect caused by the ball interacting with the water is turbulence, which causes displacement of other objects within the tank. The ball is interacting with it medium, causing a reaction.

Figure 26

Resistance of Mass

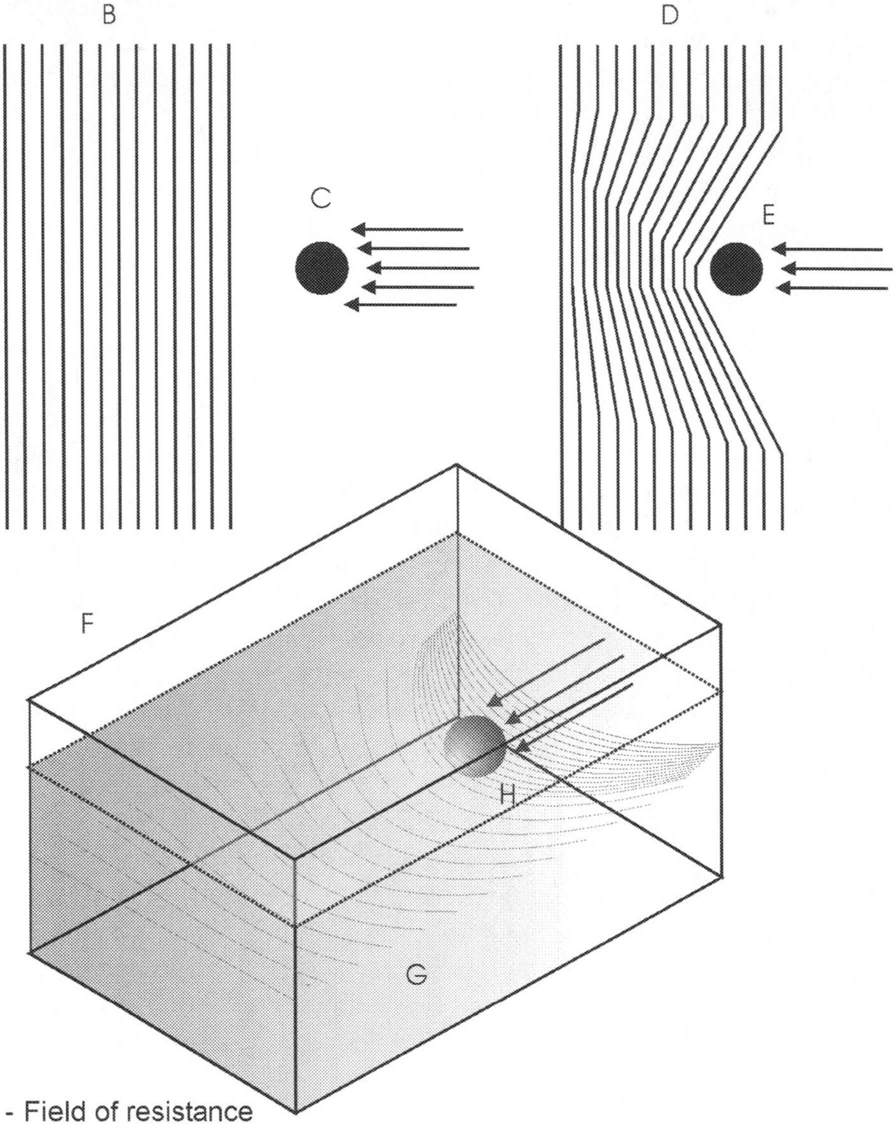

B - Field of resistance
C - Mass moving at velocity
D - Field bending and reacting to mass
F - Water tank
G - Water turbulence from ball movement
H - Ball

☐┤╟╢ Generating extreme gravitational fields involves accelerating massive objects through fields. Generating a black hole entails producing ample turbulence within the underlying fields. The object causing the turbulence should be of such mass as to create the greatest turbulence within space, thus bending universal fields that compose the fabric of space. The moving mass will induce immense drag, creating significant gravitational attraction. The resistance imposed by underlying fields will redefine the properties of the mass.

Combating the Inflationary Force

There is tranquillity in the universe as it is composed of equal halves, each with opposing properties. Every element in the universe has its equal counterpart. These elements were created as identical opposites and can merge to form the simple substance from which they originated. The original substance of the universe was created uniformly and devised out of the same primordial substance. At the beginning of time, a primordial energy was divided into two halves, and if these two halves were to ever combine, they would return back to the primordial energy. This identical division partitions all elements in the universe into opposing halves. The sustainability of these elements lies in the forces keeping them apart.

The universe is caught in a revolving cycle of change. Matter, energy, fields, and other elements are constantly interacting within a cyclical routine. Repulsive gravity is the catalyst for triggering the initial outward push of elements during the Big Bang, thereby causing the universe to inflate. A remnant of the initial push continues to propel the universe apart, while other forces form to counterbalance the inflation, thereby sustaining the cohesiveness of the universe. The universe is under a constant pressure of inflation and implosion, and struggling to sustain itself. The creation of substance, since the beginning of the universe, has introduced mechanisms in attempts to unite the universe. The introduction of novel fields, elements, and matter have been efforts in countering the destructive event that occurred at the conception of the universe.

The gravitational force struggles to combat the inflationary force caused by the Big Bang. The gravitational force is a field dedicated to uniting the universe, but is unable to consolidate its force to resist the push of inflation. The consolidated force of gravity is greater than the force of repulsion, but with matter dispersed in disproportionate quantities across the universe, the force of gravity is not potent enough to resist inflation. The forces of gravity and inflation share similar magnitudes, but are unequally distributed, making the inflationary force the dominant force over gravitational attraction. Gravity relies on the clumping of matter to exert its attractiveness. Matter is scattered about the outer edges of the universe, making the gravitational force weak and diluted. ☐─⊪ Gravity cannot combat the unified force of inflation.

When matter consolidates and clumps, it builds a gravitational field able to resist inflation. When matter clumps together, creating a strong gravitational field, it builds a force capable of pushing through the repulsion, slowing down the acceleration of matter and fields. This deacceleration creates a tunnel through space toward the tightly packed dark matter at the center of the universe. Once a tunnel is established, compressed matter interacts with antimatter, ultimately nullifying each substance. The particles located in the heavy mass, and those found within antimatter, fuse back into a substance of their original form. The two substances negate each other, and the product of this union results in the formation of the primordial substance of the universe. Figure 27 displays the relationship between the combating forces in the universe. The perimeter of the universe contains scattered matter (J) repelled by inflation (G). When matter begins to clump (B), it creates a gravity well (C), which in turn creates a tunnel (H) repelling against the forces of inflation (G). When the gravity well is strong enough, the tunnel reaches antimatter (F), and the two substances amalgamate, therein transforming into a primordial substance. The pattern of destruction and transformation continues in a cycle throughout the universe, facilitating constant agitation. The cycle continues to transform matter, thus promoting change.

| Figure 27 | Matter and Antimatter |

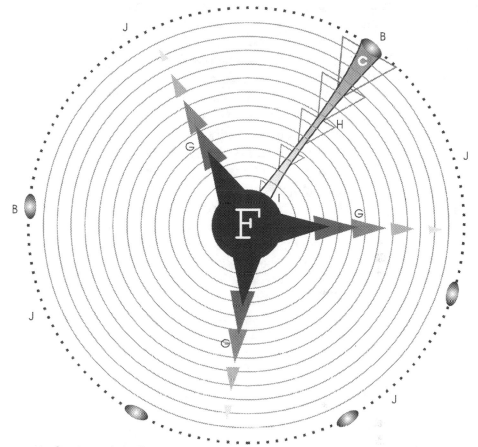

J - Scattered matter
B - Clumped matter
C - Condensed matter forming black hole
F - Antimatter
G - Repulsion force
I - Matter and Antimatter meet
H - Tunnel

Cause and Effect

The universe undergoes a series of chain reactions that produce the process of change through sequential events. Everything that changes is caused by a reaction from an event. The creation of new elements within the universe is caused by reactive events. The relationships between elements in the universe are critical to the development of the universe, as the interactions produce various degrees of reactions that promote change. Although elements are derived from the same primordial substance, they do not interact corrigibly with each other. Energy captured in matter is released when certain conditions arise through the interaction of other matter. The universe is constantly changing, rearranging elements throughout its growing process. The logic behind this process of regeneration is based on simple principles of cause and effect. A constant force is imposed upon matter within the universe, which promotes the interaction between physical objects. Constant pressure and motion contribute to the evolution of a complex universe. ⬜╫ The more pressure imposed upon substances within the universe, the more reactionary effects are caused, leading to a greater variety of elements. Pressure gives matter and the universe substance. Without constant pressure, the universe would have little substance. One of the predominant causes of pressure is gravity.

Gravity is a by-product of the interaction between matter and fields. It is a residual effect of two interacting elements, causing a warp within space. Gravity is evident when objects resist it; otherwise, we would never know that it exists. To feel the effects of gravity, you have to oppose its force. The reaction caused by matter and the underlying fields of the universe produce a hemorrhage in space in the form of an attractive force. This hemorrhaging gives rise to mass and substance, and it is a vital component for the creation of life. Gravity plays a substantial role in the metamorphosis of the universe.

Gravity is a force imposed upon matter. The source of this force lies within objects of mass, but the pulsating waves caused by gravity do not originate from matter itself. Matter does not contain an element that promotes the gravitational attractive force; rather, the effect is caused by a reaction. The reaction of mass and primordial fields gives rise to the gravitational effect. Figure 28 displays a light shining into an enclosed box, where the source of light is fixed at one end of the box and is pointed toward the opposite side. There is a hole in the wall, big enough for the head of the flashlight to project light upon the opposite wall. A ball is placed in front of the light. The effect of gravity is like the shadow projected on the opposite wall. The shadow is caused by the interaction of the flashlight with the ball. When these two elements interact, the residual effect is a dark contrast on the opposing wall. The two elements do not share a direct relationship but create a reaction when they interact.

Figure 28   Gravitational Effect

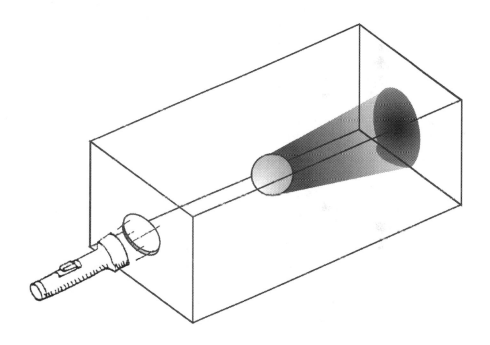

Acceleration on Earth

Gravity fields are an attractive force pulling one object toward another. Objects exerting strong gravitational forces supersede those with weak forces. Objects with minimal gravitational influence are more susceptible to being drawn toward objects exerting a stronger gravitational force. The attraction of the gravitational force draws one object directly toward another object's central force of gravity. The path that the object follows is the shortest distance toward another object or in a straight line. Objects on the surface of the Earth are drawn toward the center of the Earth, where the greatest concentration of mass resides. Objects accelerating vertically upward from Earth's surface directly contest this force and experience greater resistance. The force of gravity resists the acceleration of objects moving away from the Earth by pulling the object toward its center.

The line of gravity follows the shortest path from Point A to Point B. ▢⊦⊦⊦ An object exerting a gravitational force attracts another object along its central gravitational path. Objects moving along the central path experience the greatest gravitational effect, thereby experiencing either the attractive pull or the resisting drag. The indirect path of gravity is the parallel lanes running perpendicular to the central source of the force. Objects moving in an indirect path of gravity are accelerating perpendicular to the primary source of gravity. Substantial acceleration negates the influence of gravity. With the proper amount of acceleration, the gravitational influence imposed by a planetary object is overcome. The gravitational effect loses its intensity on objects accelerating perpendicular to the central point of gravitational influence. Resistance from gravity is experienced substantially less when accelerating horizontally along the Earth's surface, as objects are not moving in direct contrast to the central source of gravity. Traveling in parallel to the Earth's central point of gravity, alongside the emanating waves of gravity, provides a uniform resistance, which imposes less hindrance on the movement of an object.

Gravitational fields accumulate, intensify, and interact. Earth is influenced by gravitational forces from the planets within its solar system and from other foreign bodies. These foreign forces influence objects accelerating on Earth's surface. The accumulated gravitational fields from these celestial objects hinder or alleviate Earth's gravitational potency upon objects on its surface. Objects accelerating on Earth, along the central gravitational path of other planetary objects, will experience the greatest gravitational influence from these objects. Traveling toward the central gravitational path of the Sun will offset a degree of Earth's gravitational influence. The gravity from the Sun and other planetary objects affect our lateral movement on Earth as we accelerate toward or against the foreign object's central gravitational path.

Figure 29 displays the gravitational effect imposed upon objects accelerating on Earth's surface by the Sun and the Moon. The central point of the Sun's gravitational attraction (D) draws in the Earth's mass along the shortest path (F). The indirect lines of the Sun's gravitational field lie perpendicular to the shortest path or central gravitational path (F). Objects accelerating on Earth's surface are represented by solid arrows and are influenced by the gravity of the Sun, Moon, and Earth. Each planetary object retains a resistance value, which represents the force imposed upon objects when located on Earth's surface. Objects accelerating perpendicular to Earth's central gravitational path inflict half of the Earth's gravitational resistance. Scenario K aligns the Moon between the Sun and Earth. Objects accelerating away from the Earth at Point C are opposing the gravitational attraction of the Earth, Moon, and Sun combined, while objects falling toward the Earth at Point C meet no resistance. Objects accelerating from Point E oppose the gravitational force of the Earth but follow the attractive force of the Moon and Sun. Objects falling toward the Earth at Point E oppose the gravitational effects of the Sun and Moon. Objects accelerating along the central gravitational path of the Sun at Point G oppose the forces of the Sun and Moon. Objects accelerating at Point H follow the attractive force of the Sun and Moon. The optimal period of acceleration occurs when there is the least amount of resistance, and in this case it happens at Point H. Point H accelerates unparallel to Earth's central gravitational path, but follows the central gravitational path of the Moon and Sun. Scenarios J and P display events in which the Moon is located behind the Earth

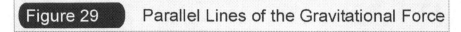

Figure 29 — Parallel Lines of the Gravitational Force

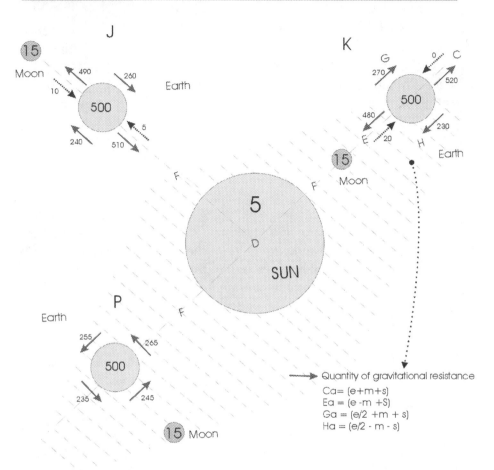

D - Central source of gravitational pull from sun
F - Shortest path of gravitational pull from sun to earth
E/C - Greatest influence by celestial objects upon earth
G/H - Parallel acceleration to earth's direct gravitational path

and to the right of the Earth in relation to the Sun. Each scenario displays the resistance points imposed by the celestial objects upon accelerating objects on Earth's surface. The objects displaying the least amount of resistance for the gravitational force accelerate with more ease.

The Purpose of Black Holes

Gravity is the agent that keeps objects rooted to Earth's surface. It is a consistent force present throughout the universe, and its effects are apparent everywhere. The force of gravity imposed by Earth adds several advantages to the objects on its surface. Its force is proportionally balanced in accordance with its mass; therefore, it does not crush objects against its surface and does not allow objects to float away into space. Gravity mitigates the structure of all things within its influence, providing uniformity to objects with mass. It provides humanity with a sanctuary on Earth by keeping its inhabitants from drifting into obscurity.

Although a saving grace, gravity does have a dark side. Extreme examples of gravity in the universe produce destructive masses called black holes. Black holes collect and clump elements with an unrelenting force, condensing matter tightly into a single point. Matter within a black hole undergoes a transformation, in preparation for its ultimate demise. Matter goes through several transformations, and when under extreme pressures, matter changes into a substance of its primordial form. This process involves returning matter to its original constituency, to a point from the beginning of time. Similar to the transformation of carbon changing into a diamond when under pressure, matter within a black hole transforms into a purified substance. Under extreme pressure, the characteristics that define matter are broken down into basic components. Pressure gives rise to change, and when matter is under extreme pressure, it changes from a physical substance into a primordial element.

Although destructive, black holes ultimately assist the universe by returning its contents back to its original form. It is a replenishing device set out to repair the damages caused by an explosive beginning. Black holes collect scattered matter, thereby recouping the essence of the universe and closing the open wound. It is a device designed to return the universe back to its former state prior to the Big Bang. Gravity's boundless force creates a mechanism able to collect scattered elements and return the universe to its original state. Gravity causes matter to congeal, thereby intensifying its attractive influence. With elements scattered throughout the universe, the gravitational force becomes deluded. The gravitational force loses the battle against the overwhelming force of inflation. Black holes are losing the struggle against the effects of the inflationary force that is expanding the universe. Inflation is dispersing elements at a greater rate than gravity can contend with. ☐┤├ Black holes lack effectiveness, as their ultimate goal to congeal all elements within the universe and return the universe to a pre-Big Bang form falters.

The life of a black hole is not infinite. When the elements that form its core evaporate, the well dries and the black hole loses its attractive force, which is required to draw in additional matter. As matter is eliminated, the mass from the black hole decreases, which lessens its gravitational influence. Left in its wake is a by-product, a primordial substance simply referred to as primal energy, which was present during the conception of the universe. This energy is the essence of the universe, a substance found in elements that make up existence. The universe is derived from uniform energy and longs to return to that initial state through devices it creates, namely black holes.

The Nature of Black Holes

Black holes are described as perforations within the fabric of reality, destroyers of existence, and the darkest mysteries of the universe. Black holes are caused by the clumping of matter to such an extent that the gravitational force creates a void in space. If the universe started from a point, then a singularity would have been the most likely candidate. The future of the universe may entail a return to a single condensed point of existence. A black hole is a mass-accumulating entity that increases its size with the addition of matter.

The name *black hole* is derived from its ability to disrupt light, trapping it when crossing its path, thereby creating the appearance of a dark void. The existence of black holes is possible given the physical principles of the universe. They play a critical role in the continuation of the universe and have been introduced at a particular stage in the progression of the universe for a purpose. The role of black holes in relation to the universe is simple yet vital to its cohesiveness. □┼╢ Black holes are the movers and destroyers of existence, as they return elements back into their original form.

The evolution of the universe has given rise to black holes. They were introduced as a device to transform existence. Black holes are devices that are capable of negating the expansion and acceleration of the universe. Gravity conflicts with the inflationary force, which is expanding the universe. The weak gravitational force gathers its strength in numbers as it collects matter, forming an immensely dense mass. With enough accumulated mass, the inflationary force fails to push the colossal clump, causing the fabric of space to stretch. The stretching of space causes a gravity well and creates a funnel through the inflationary expansion. The black hole resists the push from the inflationary force and creates an anchor in space that matter attaches itself to. The gravitational force of a black hole causes a depression in the fabric of the cosmos, which in turn creates a funnel toward the initial conception of the universe. The center of the universe is the anchor of the universe, as it contains substances that radiate a unified inflationary field.

The intensity of the gravitational force emanating from a black hole fluctuates during stages of its formation. At its conception, the black hole builds its mass and steadily increases its gravitational force. When it reaches a pinnacle mass, its resistance warps the fabric of space and creates a funnel. The destination of the funnel is matter's counterpart: antimatter. As matter and antimatter unite within the black hole, it causes a reaction, resulting in the black hole losing its mass. The fusing of the two substances negates each substance, creating a by-product of the universe's initial constituency. When enough matter is eliminated from the black hole, it loses its ability to form a tunnel and to resist the inflationary force. The repelling force of inflation

Figure 30 — Black Holes

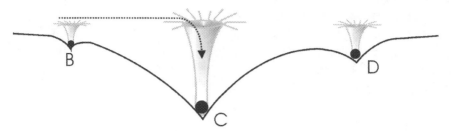

B - Black hole lesser mass
C - Black hole greater mass
D - Black hole substantial mass

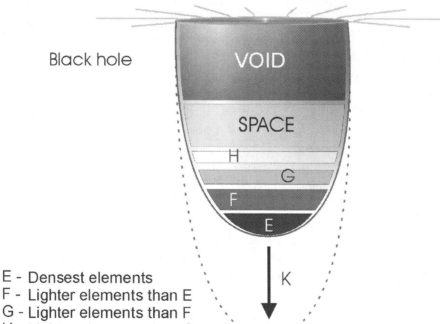

Black hole

E - Densest elements
F - Lighter elements than E
G - Lighter elements than F
H - Lighter elements than G
K - Greater weight stretches Black hole creating a tunnel

overwhelms the black hole, dispensing its mass and dispersing its gravitational force. The results of these occurrences are the mixing and dispersing of matter and energy. This cyclical process promotes change within the universe, thereby providing a device to process matter.

Black holes are the matter processing factories of the universe, caught in a cycle of collection and conversion of substance. The gravitational field emanating from the black hole creates depressions in space in order to accommodate the massive amounts of elements within it. Figure 30 displays the characteristics of a black hole. Black Hole C is a gravity well that collects matter from Black Hole B and D of lesser gravitational strength. The dominant black hole (Black Hole C) maintains the greatest mass and attracts other substances of lesser mass. The black hole consists of layers, with the densest elements (Element E) residing at the bottom or the center of the depression. The greater the mass that is collected, the greater the depression and gravitational influence (K) imposed upon the fabric of space. Transformed matter E is prepared to amalgamate with antimatter when the black hole gains enough mass to form a tunnel.

Limitless Space

> *"Space is big. You just won't believe how vastly, hugely, mind-bogglingly big it is. I mean, you may think it's a long way down the road to the chemist's, but that's just peanuts to space."*
>
> Douglas Adams (2001), The Hitchhiker's Guide to the Galaxy

The Meaning of a Medium

All objects in the universe are in motion, as all objects are influenced by time. Things that move are subject to time and exist within a medium. Mediums consist of substances that resist objects from traveling or changing at infinite speeds. They are the place holders for objects to exist in and regulate how an object exists in time. Mediums are the moderators of relationships between the universe and objects within it. They allow objects to relate and govern the conduct between objects. They are the filling in the cracks for existence, providing the universe with substance. In a logical sense, a medium is required to identify if an object exists.

Movement causes friction, a disturbance, an exchange of energy, and a change. Movement is a catalyst for destruction; there are always expenditures as a result of acceleration. Acceleration is evident when an object is perceived as moving from one point to another in relation to its medium. An object must overcome the resistance imposed by its medium, thereby causing a disturbance within the medium. An object is classified as accelerating when a reaction occurs within its resisting medium. Consider a cosmic video game where a rocket ship is spurting flames from its exhaust while sitting in the middle of a blank screen. From the ship's appearance, we would not know if it was moving. We only know that flames are emanating from its thrusters. Now add a star-filled background, the "medium." The background begins to move across the screen when the ship exhausts its flames. In relation to the background, the stars begin to pass by, and now we can say that the fixed ship in the middle of the screen is accelerating.

We know something is accelerating when the medium of that something reacts in relation to the object. A medium must exist to define movement simply because an object in empty space cannot be moving (or not moving) if its medium does not react accordingly. There would be no reference as to whether the object was moving or not. It would be uncertain if an object was traveling from Point A to Point B. The medium defines the characteristics for the movement of an object. Whether an object can move fast and how fast is determined by its medium. It also defines the limits of acceleration and movement for an object within the medium's confines. Without a resisting force, an object could move at infinite speeds, thereby eliminating time and causing the universe to begin and end in the same instance. All movement and acceleration is subject to a pace as defined by a medium, which gives rise to existence. ⊡⊣┼┤ A medium that sets a pace for existence quantifies the concept of time and the beginning of the universe.

The Observed Universe

It is difficult to believe in something that you have never seen or experienced. Discovering the mechanics of the world heavily relies upon our ability to experience the workings firsthand. Einstein's theory of gravity was not fully welcomed by scientists until he proved his theory during a solar eclipse. The way humans experience reality reflects upon their perceived reality. The perception of Earth's shape has changed throughout history due to varying human experiences. The Earth was once considered to be flat, as the vantage point for humanity during the 1600s was limited. The argument that the Earth was round in shape was not initially accepted because the Earth's entire shape could not be experienced firsthand. As humanity's perception widens, discoveries for the mechanics of existence become more prevalent and accepted.

The shape of the universe has been widely theorized but never proven, as its entirety has not been perceived. The universe has taken several forms over the centuries. Although these definitions vary, they do share some common characteristics. Experiential evidence captured by telescopes displays little logical structure in the location of stars and galaxies. From our vantage point, the universe is perceived as a flat exploding cluster. Our perception of the stars is skewed due to our limited vantage point. We perceive the universe from one vantage point, which leads us to unwavering ideas about the shape of the universe. The ability to step out of the universe to visualize its shape is beyond human capabilities. Human interaction with the universe is limited to Earth's solar system, as we cannot currently travel to distant galaxies. Humanity is limited to a two-dimensional picture of the universe that heightens our bewilderment and imagination nightly. Science ensures us that space has volume, but from Earth's perspective the solar system could well be encapsulated in a snow globe, projecting stars along its sides. The images of stars are depicted all around us, displaying no top or bottom as the entire sky is filled with twinkling lights. The galaxies continue forever with no end or beginning, and the universe seems to have no bounds in any direction. This overwhelming perspective was once held by humanity toward the Earth due to humanity's limited perception, and it continues today with the universe.

When removing the skewed partition from the universe, our galaxy finds itself on top of a bubble. Figure 31 displays the view of the universe from Earth's vantage point. From Earth's vantage point (Point E), we can perceive the stars on the other side of the universe (Position D) as light travels around the lens on the bubble (Area G). Our vantage point allows us to view every other galaxy located around the bubble due to the curvature of light (Line H) bent around the bubble by the force of gravity (Force F) generated by a central mass (Mass M). Objects within the belt of matter (Area G) are visible as their light travels through space along the "light zone" (Area G). Light pulled toward the center of the universe is not visible, as a great mass (Mass M) consumes the light, thereby creating a dark wall (Object R). The viewable light in the universe exists in the light zone (Area G), as other waves of light are pulled inward toward the dark wall (Object R). Viewing directly across the universe using the shortest path is interrupted by the dark wall (Object R).

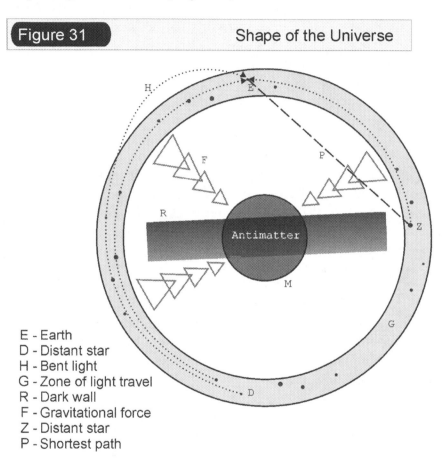

Figure 31   Shape of the Universe

E - Earth
D - Distant star
H - Bent light
G - Zone of light travel
R - Dark wall
F - Gravitational force
Z - Distant star
P - Shortest path

Stars located on the opposite end of the bubble are visible, although not directly through the center of the universe. The universe, like a sphere, reflects light around its outer edge bent by gravity. Each star's position appears at a specific location in the night sky in relation to the degree of light bending, caused by the central gravitational force. All the stars located in the light zone or "physical ring" of the universe (Area G) uniformly radiate their light against other objects within the ring. Each object within the ring perceives all other objects within the ring, although they may be on opposite ends of the universe. Light traveling from various areas around the ring create the illusion that the night sky is filled with galaxies in every direction with no bearing. For an observer on Earth, space is perceived as being widespread and abundantly overwhelmed with stars when in actuality it is limited within a designated ring. The night sky is entangled with twinkling stars that range from the next solar system to the other side of the universe. Figure 32 displays the location where starlight appears to an observer on Earth when perceiving the night sky. Starlight appearing in the northern hemisphere (Position S) comes from stars that are located near the opposite ends of the universe (Point D). Starlight appearing near the equator (Position P) comes from stars that are located relatively closer to Earth's solar system. Bent light reaches the Earth at a specific location in relation to its distance and location to Earth.

As light is bent, the true location of distant stars becomes obscured. Curving the path of light creates the illusion that an object appears farther in distance than it really is. Figure 31 displays the different distances between the direct path of an object in space and its perceived path. Light emanating from Star Z appears relatively farther than the shortest path (Path P) to the star. Calculating the distance to the star requires compensating the distortion of its light caused by the central mass (Mass M). Traveling directly to the star requires moving out of the light zone, thereby shortening the trek. □ ╫ Light distortion causes the universe to appear larger than it actually is, as objects will appear farther than they actually are.

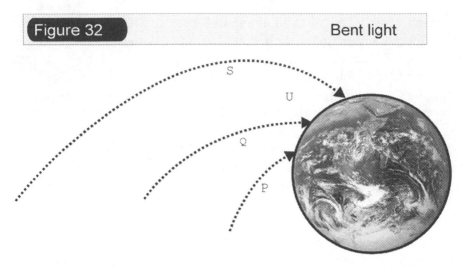

Figure 32   **Bent light**

S - Star light from opposite side of universe
Q - Star light from mid universe
P - Star light from near universe
U - Light from left side of universe

The Equation of the Universe

The code that formulates the universe is ingrained in every element that exists. Uncovering clues that help in solving this elaborate equation entails analyzing the riddle systematically by deciphering the individual components that make up the equation. You have to examine the individual parts of the equation before understanding its entirety. Examining the parts entails deciphering the micro-mechanics of the universe through the use of logic. Once a conceptual picture of the processes within the universe is contemplated, the science behind the logic can then be defined.

There are many devices in the universe that manipulate matter, including humanity. Matter consistently changes throughout the universe. To define the basic principles that drive this constant change, we need to investigate its mechanics. The universe's code is based on principles that revolve around change. It is an equation that mitigates change and that governs the process of change. One must begin from the bottom of the principle pool and investigate the simplest equations of change prior to solving the grand scheme. The search requires deciphering a general equation composed of components derived from the principles of science. We take physical principles that govern the smallest of elements, like the pieces of a puzzle, and build a foundation to reveal the underlying script. For example, apples contain seeds that contain a mechanism for an apple tree to multiply. When evaluating the conceptual idea behind the model of a fruit tree, we conclude that the tree produces apples to extend and spread the species. Taking a broader perspective of the fruit tree, we examine what the tree represents to the Earth. This requires an examination of all other tree-like species on the planet. Now continue to expand your perspective until you cannot relate the concept of the plant to any other encompassing object. This leads to the understanding of existence, as all things were created from the same origins, but instead of focusing on the concept of one subject like the tree, you must account for all subjects in the universe. The conclusions that you discover will point to one definitive purpose of existence and one definitive equation of existence.

Complex elements within the universe are compounds of simpler elements that have been amalgamated. By evaluating universal principles that influence these elements, we can derive the primary laws of the universe. All principles governing objects in the universe are joined together to make more complex laws. Together these principles form the web of reality, which encompasses the underlying fabric of reality. Principles collaborate at certain junctions to make even more complex principles. As matter changes and evolves, principles compound to reveal even more elaborate laws that govern the change of matter. As matter evolves through time, principles that govern them also evolve. ☐–ₗₗₗ The initial code of the universe has evolved into several principles required to maintain itself. Although these principles have evolved, they still contain a remnant of the original equation. To find the underlying laws of existence, you must explore these compounded principles by breaking them down into their original formulas. By reversing the complex attributions of these modern principles, one can single out the originating primal equation derived from the beginning of time. Once the basic principles are deciphered, you can form a common equation that defines the universe.

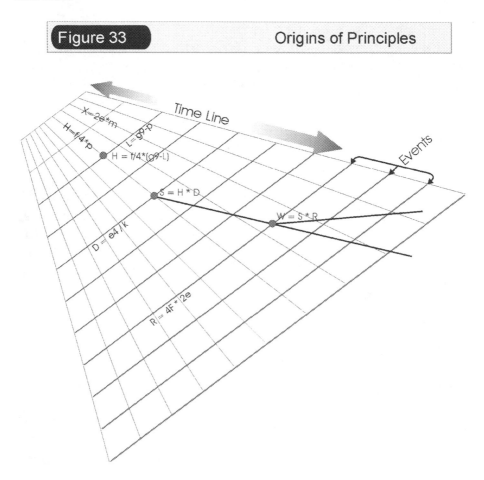

Figure 33   Origins of Principles

Figure 33 illustrates the evolution of the universal code through the universe's timeline. As time elapses, principles gain new attributes to accommodate new circumstances. The source of refined principles originates from dimensions unlike the universe. The compounding of dimensions gives rise to a variety of complex laws. The grid represents the convergence of events, causing the formation of new principles. Laws intermingle with each other to collaborate into more complex laws. For example, the initial value of H in Figure 33 branches off and transforms to become a component of the W equation.

The Universe Unravelled

> *"Everything you've learned in school as "obvious" becomes less and less obvious as you begin to study the universe. For example, there are no solids in the universe. There's not even a suggestion of a solid. There are no absolute continuums. There are no surfaces. There are no straight lines."*
>
> R. Buckminster Fuller (1895 - 1983)

The Beginning of Time

The beginning of time is synonymous with the creation of the physical universe, as one required the other to exist. The beginning of time is directly related to the creation of elements, as time is an increment of change for physical things. As soon as elements appeared into the picture, time started ticking. Time is the measurement of change, and change began when the universe suddenly expanded. The expansion of space was accompanied by fields that determined the rate of change for elements. This maximum rate became an increment of time. Time suddenly materialized through the interaction of elements and fields. The fields that govern the process of change are more commonly known as the medium of existence.

Everything that has a beginning has an end, including time, matter, and the universe. The beginning of time and the beginning of the universe are not synchronized, as the universe was once a fixed and unchanging entity absent of time. At this stage in the universe, the components that comprised time were missing, making time dysfunctional. The absence of changing elements did not require time, as time is the measurement of change and change occurs when elements contest with their medium. Time occurs when elements interact and when things change from being fixed to being in motion.

The universe is a changing entity; although time increases incrementally, its increments are fixed in length. Like the underlying fields governing the universe, time is not a component of the universe but rather exists outside it. The potential of time existed before the universe was conceived. Although time measures the changes in the universe, it does not interact with it. An increment of time is determined by fields that govern the universe. This medium, like time, exists outside the universe and was present prior to the conception of the universe. In order to manipulate time, one would have to venture beyond the dimension of the universe.

☐┤┤┤ The inception of time began from an anomaly in the universe, causing the universe to change states from being fixed to being in motion. This dramatic occurrence caused moving elements to interact with underlying fields, resulting in a residual by-product of matter, substance, and other real elements in the universe. The anomaly sparked a reaction in existence, causing primordial energy to contract and expand. The friction of energy resulted in energy taking on new forms, thereby populating the universe with substance. Figure 34 displays stages of the universe during its conception. The material universe began as an infinite unified fixed field (Image B), which began condensing (Image C) to a singular point. The excessive condensing caused exerting pressure within a singularity, causing an inflationary reaction (Image D), which caused the universe to repulse (Image E). The reaction caused an explosion as well as an implosion of elements, creating a boundary of pressure forcing elements out and pushing elements tightly in (Image E). We currently exist in the exploding wake of the Big Bang, watching the universe expand at accelerating rates.

Figure 34 — Initial state of the universe

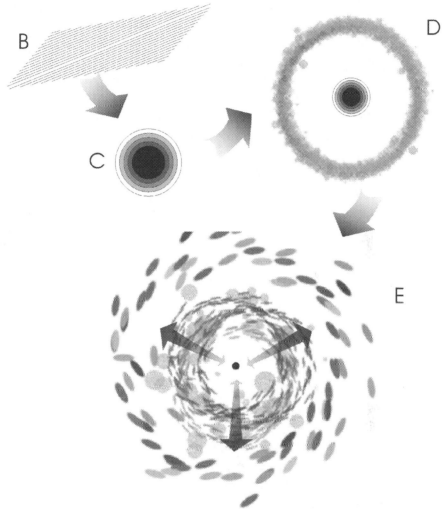

B - Initial stage of the universe, fixed waves of energy
C - Condensing fields
D - Compressed field causing an inflation
E - Repulsion of elements

The Code that Created the Universe

If you were to eliminate substance from the universe, you would be left with intangible principles. Intangible principles are the underlying universal laws that affect substance but cannot be affected by substance. These principles are mathematical truths that mitigate the conduct of physical things. They are the principles embedded into the fabric of space that impose their influence upon matter. These principles govern the material world and everything within it, including space itself. ⊡⊬ The code of the universe is encrypted with these intangible principles. The universe was conceived by these principles, caused by an anomaly, a calculated conundrum derived by infallible principles. The laws that kept the universe intact faltered and produced an irregularity. Underlying principles interact and usually fit together perfectly, but the cohesiveness of the principles suddenly failed, resulting in an ambiguity that in turn developed the equation of the universe. This obstruction caused a residual effect, which resulted in emptiness becoming something. Once the ambiguity flourished, elements interacting with the underlying fields gave the universe substance.

Anomalies are perversions of natural order. They are unique occurrences that are unexpected and depart from the norm. The basis of existence was created out of an anomaly caused by conflicting and irreconcilable principles that define the underlying laws of the universe. These principles collided, causing a remainder that resulted in the creation of substance in the universe. The universe as a result is an anomaly, an obscured occurrence at a brief moment. This anomaly occurred in one instance, and every instance after that entailed a process designed to reverse the effects of the anomaly. The principles that keep the universe intact are now struggling to keep it together. These principles are the blueprints of how the universe recovers from the anomaly. The universe continues to transform in accordance to these principles, aiming at absolving itself of the freak occurrence. The healing process began after the conception of the universe and continues to this present instance.

Traveling in east Russia, you're never surprised at the multitude of languages and cultures you'll come across. The invention of language is unique in every village, as each language is slightly augmented by local cultural influences. Throughout history, the human species has developed complex languages, resulting in cultural segregation. Among these diversities, there is one universal language that is shared among cultures: mathematical principles. Cultures have understood the meaning of basic mathematics as it relates to commerce. It was essential that tribes abide by these principles because it governed their daily lives. Monetary transactions are conducted daily in the marketplace by people of different cultures and languages, but the principles of mathematics that are applied to these transactions are identical. The mastery of these universal truths creates some commonality between the cultures and their trade. It introduces a common understanding of things beyond their own secluded circle. These principles will not only unite foreign cultures, they will unite the universe itself.

No matter how diverse the culture, the principles of mathematics becomes the common language that widens the window of comprehension. This methodical plot leading humanity is by design. We are prescribed to learn the principles of mathematics because mathematics holds the underlying logic required to lead humanity toward its ultimate objective. The mastery of mathematics and universal truths provides humanity with the means to solve the universe's anomaly. This universal language holds the secrets of the beginning of the universe and ultimately its code. When all subjective human traits are shed, mathematical principles will reveal the underpinnings of a complex universe.

The Lifecycle of the Universe

The universe evolves in stages. Stages represent significant leaps within an entity's growth and its compliance with its medium. The progression and maturity of the universe is synonymous with its evolutionary transformation. The universe has transposed several evolutionary stages, with each successive stage requiring less time to achieve. The rate of evolution in the universe is increasing, meaning that the evolutionary process is occurring at a faster pace. The more elaborate and complex substances are within the universe, the greater the amount of transformations there are of elements, resulting in an accelerated rate of evolution. The complexity of elements existing on the edges of the universe gives rise to more complex elements that change at a greater pace. Matter has great tendencies to change when situated in an environment that promotes change.

An essential part of understanding the universe is determining which evolutionary stage it presently resides in. Understanding this concept allows us to decipher the makeup of the universe during its early infancy, thereby determining its potential future. Initial perceptions of the universe gave scientists a close approximation of its age. Scientists detected a red shift from radio waves emanating from deep space and used this data to calculate the age of the universe. There are several ways to determine the age of an object on the surface of the Earth, one being simple observation. Understanding the current universe's evolutionary stage requires a broader perspective of the spectrum of stages. Observing patterns in evolutionary stages allows scientists to piece together probable future scenarios of the universe. Early stages provide evidence that science can measure and examine, allowing for future stages to be systematically calculated. This task entails gathering patterns to predict a definite conclusion for the final stages of the universe. The universe is a complex entity, constantly changing to improve on its previous stage, including the transformation of elements that exist within it. Humanity, being a critical part of the universe, is automatically incorporated into this process.

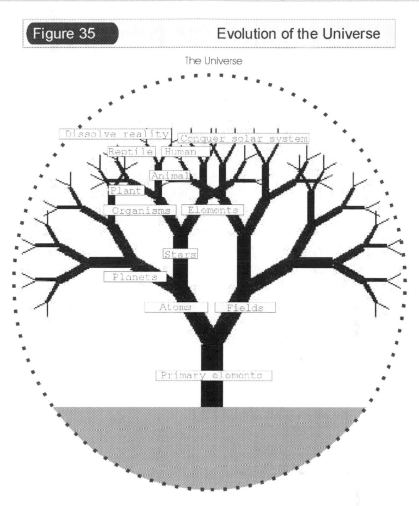

Figure 35   Evolution of the Universe

The human species represents a stage of the universe's evolution, but there lingers a beckoning question of exactly which stage that is? Understanding the universe's evolution requires an understanding of its relationship with humanity. The universe's evolution has grown in conjunction with the evolution of Earth and its inhabitants. The process of evolution is encoded in all things in existence, including humanity. The universe has surpassed the stage of introducing conscious beings to explore and repair itself. Humanity therefore represents a critical stage in the universe's evolution. The introduction of self-aware beings with the ability to question existence was a vital evolutionary leap for the universe. The subsequent stages of the universe's evolution have been replaced by humanity's evolutionary prowess. ☐–╫ Humanity's stages of progression and evolution represent the subsequent stages in the universe's evolution. The universe's sequential evolutionary stages are inherited by humanity's progression and are aligned with stages in which human beings become masters of their environment. Humanity has taken over the forthcoming leaps of the universe's evolution and has become a representation of the universe's sequential advancements. These leaps lapse in shorter intervals as the rate of evolution accelerates under the direction of humanity. Figure 35 displays the tree of the universe's evolutionary path, which is in line with humanity's progress. As the evolutionary process becomes man-made, the sequential steps of the universe's progression include humans mastering their environment, including Earth, the solar system, galaxy systems, and reality itself. As humanity advances and becomes more proficient, it creates its own man-made evolution kindled by the will instilled within the human code. Just as the branches on the tree get finer, so do the stages of human progression and ultimately the universe's evolution.

The Intelligence in the Universe

A clock is an intricate device that works with precision and form. To say that a clock has intelligence would be incorrect, and the same can be said about the universe. The universe is a precise calculative device, an automatic mechanism that produces output based on calculations. These calculations are derived from inputs contingent upon physical laws that govern them. The universe is unable to contemplate logical thought, just as a clock cannot self-adjust for Daylight Savings. The universe is a perfectly synchronized device that changes based on precise calculations.

Evidence of the universe's mechanics is found throughout nature and in space. Humanity exists in a perfectly programmed device conditioned upon physical principles. Although evidence of this logical structure is abundant in the universe, it is not readily apparent. Humans have a misconceived perception of nature as being chaotic.

Nature has produced examples of extreme intellectual design that can be found throughout existence. These intricate designs reveal themselves as being part of a grand scheme conducted by a mechanism. Each discovery reveals a grand conceptualized plan orchestrated by a supreme device.

Intelligence in the universe exists within its offspring, namely humans. Humans are a component of the grand scheme, designed as thought processing vehicles. The universe has systematically created a creature to process thought, thereby utilizing retained memory. Humans are a calculative device and an important component of the mechanics for the universe. The universe's calculating mechanisms have led to the production of such a creature in order to advance itself toward sequential developmental phases. Consider humanity as a fine gear in a watch, designed to complete the grand scheme of telling time. Although a minimal component within the watch, humanity is a critical component in the grand scheme of telling time. The inevitability of a conscious being within the universe was a foregone conclusion. ☐–⫫ Humans are a process within several trillion processes designed to operate as a mechanism for the universe.

The Universe Is Finite

There are two distinctions of existence: things that are infinite and things that are finite. Objects with infinite attributes have always existed and are fixed. Objects of finite existence are things that can change. The universe exists on several planes that are finite and infinite. There is a hierarchy of supporting structures that comprise the rules on how existence operates. Each supporting plane is layered one after another like a layered cake, with the bottom planes regulating the rules for the top planes. Attributes from each layer influence the attributes of the layers above them. This relational chain of influence cannot transcend backwards toward underlying plateaus. The plateaus supporting the universe formulate the physical laws that govern the universe. These planes have always existed in an intangible state since the conception of the universe and cannot be influenced. The universe is a changing entity; therefore, it is finite in quantity and duration. □—╫ The universe has a definite beginning and end, as all changing elements do.

The more you correlate the universe as being an organism rather than an inanimate structure, the more you understand its significance. The universe is a living, evolving organism, which was conceived from nothingness and will return to nothingness. The mechanisms that started the universe exist outside the universe. The universe acquires its attributes from several underlying plateaus that are infinite. Changing time allows for the universe to grow in increments. The universe is growing and aging, and has a limited life span. The friction caused by the Big Bang has left the universe in a precarious state as it attempts to break out of its condition by building devices to return to its former fixed state. The initial fixed state of the universe was absent of turmoil and change. It was a state of wholeness and compliance. The consciousness of the universe is instilled into humanity, as humanity holds the same desire of achieving completeness and unity. Humanity is an extension of the universe and is instilled with primal instincts to carry out the desire for completeness, which are notions identical to the objectives of the universe.

Creation within the Universe

"The only thing that scares me more than space aliens is the idea that there aren't any space aliens. We can't be the best that creation has to offer. I pray we're not all there is. If so, we're in big trouble."

Ellen DeGeneres (1982)

Other Earth-Like Planets

Supporting life within the universe requires a specific combination of elements and abundant planning. Earth is a combination of several elements amalgamated with precise measurements enabling it to support life. Life is a rare commodity in the universe and requires unique arrangements of specific elements. The abundance of these elements located within the vicinity of a life-bearing planet is vital. Earth attained most of its elements from its own solar system. Some of these life-bearing elements are water, gases, carbon, and so on. The abundance of these elements found in Earth's solar system gives rise to the possibility of life. Without the proper quantity of unique elements in Earth's solar system, life would not be possible.

There are other planets like Earth within the universe. In order to compose a planet similar to Earth, you must have the precise amount of life-bearing elements located in surrounding planets like those found in Earth's solar system. The proximity of these elements to the life-bearing planet would be similar to Earth's proximity to its neighboring planets. Several conditions dictate the creation of life and many revolve around the configuration of the planet's environment. Favorable conditions for the environment alone would not suffice, as life requires a more majestic arrangement. The formation of Earth was brought upon by the mixture of elements found on other planets within its solar system. ⬜┤┤┤ The ingredients for Earth are found in planets circulating around in its solar system. Gases similar to those found in Jupiter, rocks like those on Mars, and liquid like those found on Pluto are ingredients found on Earth that make it hospitable. The early stages of Earth's solar system comprised of a melting pot of elements, which separated into solitary satellites. When Earth's solar system cooled, the mixtures fused, creating a delicate blend, thereby forming a planet that was hospitable. Earth's solar system gave rise to a life-bearing planet given the precise amount of ingredients it contained. A solar system similar to that of the Earth would be required for the possibility of supporting life.

In order to create another Earth like planet, you require planets bearing similar elements within a solar system similar to that of Earth. The planets must bear elements of equal abundance and size to those planets within Earth's system. Even the star that brings warmth to the planet must be of similar size and distance from the life-bearing planet. A duplicate solar system with the same elements as Earth would be the requirement for the opportunity of life. Although Earth's solar system is a rare ensemble in the universe, a duplicate system would not be improbable.

Life on Other Planets

Creating an ideal and hospitable planet similar to that of Earth requires a unique combination of elements coming together within a precise frame of time. The chances of these unique elements converging are rare, but they occurred during a period of the universe's inflation. From scientific observations, we see a cesspool of cosmological activity, but as the elements of the universe expand, the opportunity for the correct elements converging and creating the circumstances for a life-bearing planet becomes less probable. The timing for the formation and incubation of life is limited to a point in time where the universe's elements have interacted with such abundance during a specific stage of the universe's growth.

There are certain stages within the universe's development that produced an environment for the creation of life. Life requires certain elements to converge at precise measurements, similar to that of a recipe. These elements are scattered throughout the universe. Some galaxies may have an abundance of one element but lack another. Therefore, the interaction of planets, stars, and galaxics is vital for the creation of life. The more interactions there are between stellar objects within the universe, the greater the probability of life forming in the universe. As the universe expands, the availability of stellar objects converging becomes less probable. The probability of life forming diminishes as the universe grows and disperses.

Timing is crucial for the opportunity of life. The recipe of life requires a vast array of elements to converge in a single area. These elements are complex and have evolved during certain stages of growth in the universe. These elements were not available during the early stages of the universe. The variety of elements required for life took time to form and evolve into what they are today. ▢┼┼┼ The maturity of the universe is vital to the formation of life, as the elements required for life had to be created. The complexities of elements within the universe gave rise to the variety of life. The abundance of these elements were present during later stages of the universe. The opportunities for life during the early stages and later stages of the universe were dismal.

Figure 36 displays the window of opportunity for the creation of life during the expansion of the universe. Elements required for the creation of life were not available during the initial stages of the universe (Point S). The timing of elements converging during later stages of the universe (Point P) is not ideal for the creation of life. The window of opportunity resides around a single area (Area C), where the necessary elements, the universe's maturity, and the expansion of the universe meet the required conditions. The necessary elements came together at a certain point in time, allowing for the opportunity of life to occur. A certain stage of the universe's growth introduces

Figure 36   Probability of Another Earth

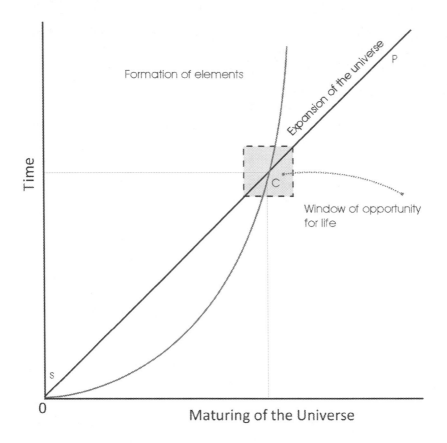

C - Certain stage of the universe when the proper combination of elements converged as the universe expanded.

these elements in order to produce life. The window of opportunity for the creation of a life-bearing planet is within this time frame. The search for other life in the universe should focus on planets that are of the same age as that of Earth. The probability of discovering other life in the universe is at its highest when searching for systems that were formed at a certain time frame during the universe's growth.

Probability of Other Life

It would be rare to find life in the universe similar to life here on Earth. The likelihood of discovering life increases when searching within an area where life already exists (or once existed). ☐╌╫╌ Life has a likelihood to exist where other life can be found. Life requires a combination of several elements that exist in a solar system that is known to have life. There is a greater degree of success of discovering life on other planets when studying planets in Earth's solar system. Those planets closest to Earth are more likely to contain remnants of life.

There is evidence of life on Mars because Mars is a congenial component of Earth's life-bearing attributes. The formation of Earth required an abundant source of hard materials located in a solar ring around the Sun, at a specific distance from the Sun. Earth and Mars share common attributes of life-bearing substances, which complement each planet. Discoveries that imply that Mars had the makings of another Earth are valid simply due to its proximity to Earth. The lively state of Earth is not an anomaly in comparison to other planets in its solar system. Life's abundance on Earth dictates the possibility of life existing in the surrounding systems. Earth's solar system is a lively system; the odds that life exists anywhere else than Earth diminishes as you travel farther away from Earth's solar system. Earth's solar system has proven to contain the conditions necessary for life. Those systems in relation to Earth's system have a higher probability of containing the elements required to support life rather than those farther away. The possibility of other life is contingent upon a planet's proximity to Earth's solar system.

The rarity of discovering the unique combination of elements required to produce life within the universe is immense. Life is scarce in the universe because the odds of combining the correct elements to produce life are not good. The elements required to produce life cannot be found uniformly throughout the universe. The fixed amount of elements required for life originated from a single source during the conception of matter, and they were dispersed unequally during the expansion of the universe. Locating the source of the dispersal for these elements is vital in identifying viable planets that are life-bearing. Earth's solar system originated from these elements, and tracking Earth's origins will identify other systems that originated from the same source. Earth's solar system gradually evolved from one area, and other systems originating from that area may contain similar elements to maintain life.

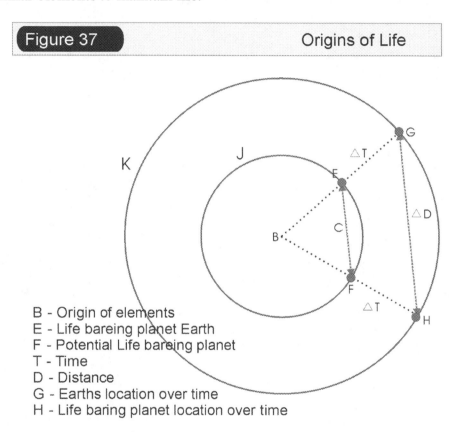

Figure 37   Origins of Life

B - Origin of elements
E - Life bareing planet Earth
F - Potential Life bareing planet
T - Time
D - Distance
G - Earths location over time
H - Life baring planet location over time

Elements required to sustain life on Earth were acquired from a source in which other solar systems have evolved. Figure 37 displays a chart explaining the origins of life. The elements required to sustain life originated from a central area (Point B) and over time, expanded to Phase J, where life began on Earth (Point E). Other planets (Planet F) originating from elements of the origin of life-bearing elements (Point B) have a higher potential of sustaining life. As phases change (Phase K) through the passing of time, the distances of life-bearing planets

(Planet G, Planet H) increase uniformly. Other life-bearing planets are identified by mapping their origins to Earth's origins. Locating these planets involves measuring their trajectory and travel distance from the origin of the life-bearing source (Point B).

| Figure 38 | Stages of the Universe |

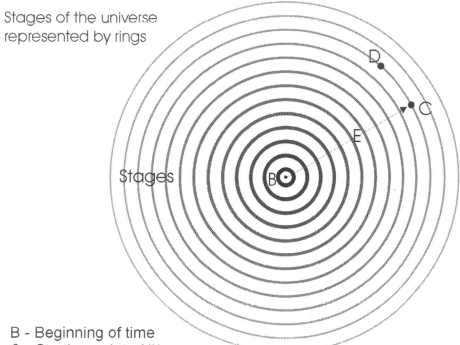

Stages of the universe represented by rings

Stages

B - Beginning of time
C - Starting point of life
D - Stage and ring where life exists
E - Time required for elements to mature.

Tracking the stage of the universe when life began is vital in detecting other life within the universe. The probability of life forming occurred at a certain window of time where the universe had conformed into a specific state that allowed for the sustainability of life. The maturity of the universe dictates when elements were available in order to sustain life. These elements have evolved and converged at a certain point in the universe's growth. The creation of these elements occurred during a stage of the universe's growth. This

223

unique stage possessed the initial opportunity for life to form. Identifying this stage and sequential stages marks the time where the universe was capable of sustaining life. These stages identify the age of opportunity for the creation of life. Figure 38 displays the increments of the universe's progressive stages. The total time required for life to begin in the universe is the amount of stages starting from the beginning of time (Point B) to the conception of life (Point C). All planets within Stage D have a greater possibility to sustain life, as the elements required to sustain life were available at that point in time. Elements at this stage have evolved to a degree where the creation of life was possible. The progressive stages of the universe's evolution gives rise to elements that produced life.

Changing Existence

> *"One, a robot may not injure a human being, or through inaction,*
> *allow a human being to come to harm;*
> *Two, a robot must obey the orders given it by human beings*
> *except where such orders would conflict with the First Law;*
> *Three, a robot must protect its own existence as long as such*
> *protection does not conflict with the First or Second Laws."*
>
> Isaac Asimov (1920 - 1992), Laws of Robotics from I. Robot, 1950

Controlling the Chaotic Universe

When we look at the night sky, there is no apparent symmetry or logic in the location of stars. Examining the universe closer reveals stars, galaxies, and matter moving farther away from each other at an explosive rate. Elements within the universe are spreading outwardly with increasing velocities in relation to each other. There is every indication that the universe is expanding from a central point. The universe originated from a repulsion of elements, which continues to disperse matter across space.

An explosion by any means is not perceived as orderly, but rather chaotic and disorganized. Yet the laws governing this chaotic event are anything but disorganized. Universal laws of motion, acceleration, and matter contain profound logic that renounce the concept of chaos existing in this established order. Order and disorder are opposing factions, and both cannot exist harmoniously. Chaos and order can exist linearly, isolated from one another, but one faction cannot exist within the other. One of these conditions does not belong in the universe, and the indicators within existence are pointing toward one dominant conclusion. The underlying principles and laws that govern the universe are structured and are based on logic. Logic to any degree gives rise to order, and order can be found uniformly throughout the universe. Evidence of order in the universe outweighs the theories that encapsulate the universe in a chaotic state. The dominant underlying basis throughout the universe reflects upon order, and chaos has no place within it.

If chaos existed in the universe, it existed at a point where order did not exist. Only the randomness of chaotic obscurity could have developed a random event in the absence of order. The state of existence was once held in the obscurity of chaos, where the principles of the underlying structure of existence were nonexistent. The universe began out of obscurity and then transformed into order. The chaotic beginnings of the universe gave rise to order in an attempt to reverse its chaotic beginning. Since the creation of the universe, order has been enlisted to negate the occurrence of chaos, which has thrown the universe into obscurity. In order to repel the destruction caused by chaos, structure has been introduced. An ordered existence continues to compound, as structure matures and becomes more prevalent. The universe was not prepared for the introduction of chaos, but has steadily increased its stature with order to repel the chaos. Time is an ally of order, as order increases in strength with time. Uniformed structure will once again prevail by gaining the means to reverse the actions of chaos. ☐┤┼┤ The transformation of the universe has been a change from chaos to order.

The chaos we perceive in the universe is dependent upon the order that governs it. Although the explosion of elements is a natural phenomena of the universe, it is in contrast to its founding order. The universe is out of control and needs to return to normalcy. This observation of disorder is mutual among humans, as we are coached to be organized and follow the notion of order. Humanity has evolved out of disorder by design. The progression of humanity involves formatting disorder into ordered structure. Similarly, the universe began out of a chaotic state and now subsides into order. The universe was created from disorder and is now taming its turbulent beginnings with order.

Humans are orderly creatures by design. Humanity develops social laws, principles, and civil societies that pave a process for controlling chaos. A sense of order is instilled within humanity in order to shun disorder and chaos. Chaos is perceived as a perversion of civilization, which depreciates human progress. The will of man is ingrained with a sense of order, and the process of eliminating chaotic persuasions assists human progress. When we observe the universe inflating out of control, we naturally see this disorder as an anomaly that needs to be corrected. As the responsibility of the universe becomes more that of humanity's, humans will inevitably take on the burden of restoring order in the universe. The motives have been instilled in the will of man, encompassing an automatic calling for a task fitting for humans.

The struggle against chaos is a continuous feat. As the human species progresses, humanity cultivates nature, transforming it into resources. Humanity's forte is to transform environments into hospitable domains. As humanity's environment grows beyond Earthly limits, it will cultivate new terrain, thereby eliminating chaos unconsciously along the way. Planets, solar systems, and galaxies will be transformed into uniformed domains, thereby creating a wave of order. Humanity will spread its influence, systematically transforming the universe into a uniformed structure. Humanity's conquest to restore order will occur automatically, driven by the human will to cultivate energy. Man will not recognize his actions as those assisting the universe; rather, they will be of his will for his own motives. The cultivation of nature for humanity continues until the farthest reaches of the universe have been transformed.

Relationships Between Elements

The universe consists of components that work together like clockwork. There are relationships between vital elements in the universe that are complementary to each other. The absence of a vital component in the universe displaces the ability of the universe to function. In order for the universe to function, it requires interrelated elements to operate in unison. The harmony of the universe rests on the relationships of elements that reside within it.

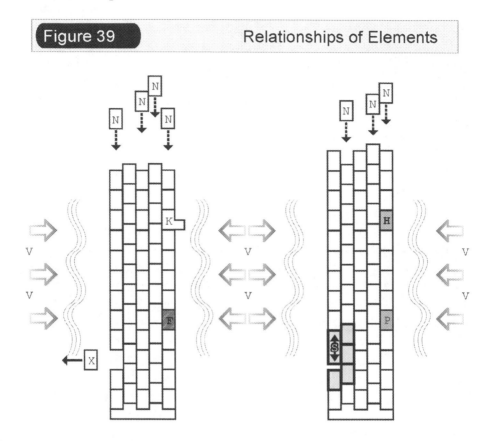

Figure 39   Relationships of Elements

X - Component which has been dislodged
K - Inefficient component
F - Porous component
N - New components building the structure

There is a hierarchy of dependable relationships among elements within the universe. Several elements depend upon the availability of other elements in order to exist. This relationship is a one-to-many association, with the contingent elements located at the base of the pyramid supporting complementary elements above. The base of the pyramid contains the underlying substance critical to sustaining dependent substances. Removing one element from the hierarchy destabilizes the structure of the pyramid and places dependent elements at risk of extinction. For instance, life cannot exist without matter, and matter cannot exist without gravity. ☐─╫╢ The universe is a highly efficient mechanism that continually strives to be structurally sound. It is a mechanism that is constantly refining to improve on its efficiency. Dysfunctional components are weeded out and are either redesigned or replaced. Figure 39 is an interpretation of the components in the universe cooperating within a structure. As the universe grows with time, it creates new components (component N). These new components rely upon existing components located at the foundation of the structure. The efficiency of the structure is constantly tested by external forces (Force V), ensuring that the structure sustains optimality. If a component (Component X) should be removed from the structure, the surrounding components would be reinforced. Component X would be compensated for by another component (Component S), thereby maintaining the integrity of the structure. Components (Component K) that infringe on the efficiency of the structure are removed and replaced by an optimal component (Component H). Components (Component F) that lack functionality within the structure are amended (Component P). The stability of the structure stays intact with the constant refinement of its components. This process ensures that the structure will prevail with optimality. The processes of efficiency found in organisms on Earth are the same processes that have been at work in the universe since its conception. The universe operates with similar motives, equal to those found in simple organisms on Earth. The mechanics of the universe can be represented by the simple processes of optimality found throughout existence.

Variety in the Universe

Variety is a mannerism of life, and uniqueness is a virtue of matter. The variety of elements throughout the universe allows for the continuous formation of unique substances. The variety of substances has been brought about by universal progression. As time advances, universal progression promotes the variety of substances. Matter reinvents itself through the passage of time, combining elements with distinct combinations, thereby forming novel substances. The universe is constantly reinventing itself, mixing elements and creating new substances. This process of continuous mixing has carried on to such an extent that the cosmos appears unique in every direction. ☐─╫ Objects in the universe are like snowflakes; no two clusters, systems, or planets are identical.

Time gives rise to change. The greater the time elapsed, the more change that occurs. Change ushers in variety as matter contorts into unique combinations. The combination of unique substances gives rise to even more uniqueness in the universe. The variety of elements within the universe promotes the unique formation of future substances. Substances that are exceptionally unique are derived from distinct elements, as there is a greater possibility of uniqueness given a combination of distinct elements. As time progresses, the variety and uniqueness of elements within the universe increase. The diversification of the universe relies upon the variety of present elements and time.

Although matter is limited in quantity, it is not limited in variety, given time. The underlying principles governing the universe are based on calculations and the manipulation of numbers, which have no bounds. The universe is founded on a code that processes infinite numerical calculations when given infinite numerical inputs, which gives rise to endless possibilities. Numbers, like the opportunity of unique elements, continue indefinitely. The code behind the design of matter utilizes endless numbers, creating a pool of unlimited design. As numbers progress, distinct formulations are produced over time. The infinite numbers injected into the code of existence give rise to infinite possibilities.

The Curvature of a Medium

Einstein illustrated a universe with curves and divots in space time, which create an attractive force of gravity. These divots are created by matter floating within a medium of fields, causing space to warp. Slow moving and bulky matter stretches space, creating pockets in which other matter gets sucked into. Photons, particles that move at high velocities, do not emit a gravitational attraction and do not create divots in space. Particles that do not create a gravitational field are moving at the pace of the underlying medium of the universe. They move with the wave of fields, thereby not creating a disturbance in space time. We can experience these particles, as they are within the speed limits of the universe's medium. Universal fields pulsate at a frequency, and matter that exists within this frequency can be experienced by human senses. Matter retains substance when it exists within the confines of the universal medium.

The faster a particle moves within the universal medium, the fewer attributes it retains. Photon particles are simple particles with little substance. A photon particle accelerates at the same pace as the underlying fields of the universe, thereby allowing the photon to retain a simplistic form. A section of space time that contains only photon particles is flat and smooth, and does not contain divots or protrusions. Particles that move quicker than the medium of the universe create an opposite effect, compared to those particles moving slowly in space. If a particle moves quicker than the underlying fields, it creatures an outward or upward protrusion in the fabric of space. Space time would warp outwardly, creating a hill instead of a divot. This hill in the fabric of space exerts a repulsion effect instead of an attractive force. Matter located within the vicinity of this type of particle will be repulsed at an intensity of the particle's velocity above the limiting frequency of the underlying fields. Figure 40 displays two elements, one moving within the frequency of the universal fields (Object B), and one accelerating beyond the frequency (Object A). Matter moving within the speed limit of the medium of space emits a gravitational effect by creating a divot in space. Particles moving faster than the medium of space emit an inflationary repulsion effect that repulses matter. For example, a ball rolling on a sheet of cloth with mounds protruding from the cloth will move away from the mounds toward divots. This illustration for the fabric of space is curvy, containing divots and hills.

Figure 40   Experience Medium

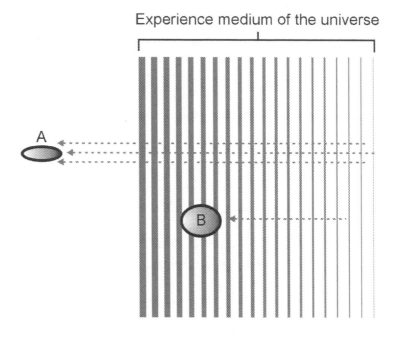

A - Elements outside the medium of the universe
B - Matter that can be experienced

The frequency range for the medium of the universe represents the proverbial surface for the fabric of space. Every particle that exists on or below the surface can be experienced by humans. ▢┤╫╫ Particles moving beyond the frequency of the medium cannot be experienced and create a dark void known as dark matter. Figure 41 illustrates the frequency range for the medium of the universe and those particles that move at a pace outside that frequency. Particles moving quicker than the medium appear to be dark, as they cannot reflect light that exists within the medium of the universe. Light particles do not move fast enough to reflect off of dark particles moving at greater velocities. For instance, a fish can experience objects in water (its medium) and not those things above the water's surface. Objects beyond the water's surface will not be directly experienced.

Figure 41   Dark Matter

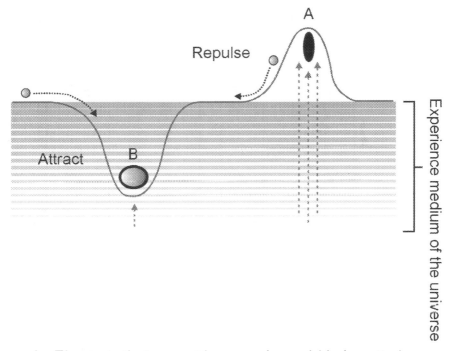

A - Elements that cannot be experienced (dark matter)
     Elements moving faster than the medium of existence
B - Matter in a gravity well

Part 4 Discover your nature

This book is a guide to uncover your true nature, a series of texts designed to open your perspective to logical existence. Some of us reach that enlightenment through different channels, and in the context of the *Automatic Universe*, some reach this destination by coursing through certain chapters. Below is your own personal entry log for the steps you've taken reaching a pinnacle awareness. Record the sections you have selected in **Subject Keys** into the Path to discovery chart below. This chosen path was your sacred journey of enlightenment. Some have shared the same path that you have followed and have felt similar emotions along that journey. This is an opportunity for you to share your journey with others and to discover the reasons for your selection.

Enter the numbers into our website to view insights into your nature.

Path to discovery   www.AutomaticUniverse.com

Journey 1

page number							

Journey 2

page number							

Journey 3

page number							

Bibliography

Allen, Thomas B. *Vanishing Wildlife of North America*. Washington, D.C.: National Geographic Society, 1974.

Boorstin, Daniel J. *The Creators: A History of the Heroes of the Imagination*. New York: Random, 1992.

Hall, Donald, ed. *The Oxford Book of American Literacy Anecdotes*. New York: Oxford UP, 1981.

Searles, Baird, and Martin Last. *A Reader's Guide to Science Fiction*. New York: Facts on File, Inc., 1979.

Toomer, Jean. *Cane*. Ed. Darwin T. Turner. New York: Norton, 1988.

"Azimuthal Equidistant Projection." *Merriam-Webster's Collegiate Dictionary*. 10th ed. 1993.

Pettingill, Olin Sewall, Jr. "Falcon and Falconry." *World Book Encyclopedia*. 1980.

Tobias, Richard. "Thurber, James." *Encyclopedia Americana*. 1991 ed.

Hall, Trish. "IQ Scores Are Up, and Psychologists Wonder Why." *New York Times* 24 Feb. 1998, late ed.: F1+.

Kalette, Denise. "California Town Counts Down to Big Quake." *USA Today* 9 21 July 1986: sec. A: 1.

Kanfer, Stefan. "Heard Any Good Books Lately?" *Time* 113 21 July 1986: 71-72.

Trillin, Calvin. "Culture Shopping." *New Yorker* 15 Feb. 1993: 48-51.

Groups and Information

Visit **AutomaticUniverse.com** to interact with groups, schools, forums, questions and answers, videos, and more.

For press inquires please email Jeffrey@AutomaticUniverse.com
Requests for book signings please email
Jeffrey@AutomaticUniverse.com

Visit me through the following online accounts:

Twitter	**AutomaticU**
Facebook	**AutomaticU**
YouTube	http://www.youtube.com/AutomaticU
Email	Jeffrey@AutomaticUniverse.com
Website	**www.AutomaticUniverse.com**

Book Cover

A special thank you to all of our supporters.

A Guru's Perspective of the Universe

The Automatic Universe continues with the next
book in the series with A Guru's Perspective of the Universe. Get
ground breaking revelations about existence through the eyes of a
guru. Acquire this book and the Automatic Universe through our
website www.AutomaticUniverse.com

Order Online

Our products are
available at
www.AutomaticUniv
erse.com

A Guru's Perspective of the Universe

From the author of "The Automatic Universe"